MUSICAL THEATRE
CHOREOGRAPHY

In memoriam: Robert Allen
Berger. Thanks for this show.

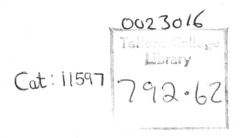

This edition first published in Great Britain 1990 by A & C Black
(Publishers) Limited, 35 Bedford Row, London WC1R 4JH

ISBN 0-7136-327-9

Copyright © 1990 by Helen Vidockler

A CIP catalogue record for this book is available from the British
Library.

Originally published in the U.S.A. 1990 by Back Stage Books, an
imprint of Watson-Guptill Publications, a division of Billboard
Publications, Inc., 1515 Broadway, New York, NY 10036

Printed in U.S.A.

To Deborah Schlehlein, to carry the torch

ACKNOWLEDGMENTS

I t is not possible to thank every teacher, student, performer, or audience member who, by example or presence, provided the sum experience necessary for this work. I hope that these people will find here something they have contributed, and that the insights they helped generate will help many to better enjoy, and to better stage, musical comedy. There is, after all, a method to the madness.

Special thanks to Emile Capouya, for his vision when there was barely more than an outline; Jolita Rouson, for all her efforts; Carlin Long, for being there as the best of friends during the worst of times; and Peggy McGlone of Waltham, Massachusetts, for sharing her system of dance notation.

Thanks also to Donald MacLaren, for his judgment and professional guidance in presenting the manuscript; Scott Shettleroe, for his skilled and critical help with the music excerpts; Robert Franklin and Virginia Tobiassen of McFarland & Co., for being confident, concerned, and cooperative; Tad Lathrop of Back Stage Books, for making it happen; Fred Weiler of Back Stage Books, for helping to turn the manuscript into a book; and, most of all, Helen Vidockler, who kept everything moving, and without whom this project would not have been completed.

CONTENTS

INTRODUCTION

ach year, in towns and cities across the United States,
virtually *every* high school, college, and community theater group presents a revival of a popular musical comedy. Inherently American, musicals enjoy consistent success,
bringing pleasure to viewers and participants alike. And because of the ongoing national interest in dance, properties
with a dancing emphasis are being staged locally with increasing frequency. Non-professional groups are now apt to
want to include the major dance sequences contained in these
shows rather than omit them.

The choreographer is in a unique position. While the
director has the given script to work from, and the musical
director teaches music and songs already written, the choreographer must undergo a specific process to first *create* his
material, structuring his dances to suit the dramatic context,
and finalizing the steps to be used even before they can be
taught to performers.

In amateur situations, the person assigned to this task
may have a limited theatrical background—or none at all. If
trained in classical or other formalized dance, he would still
have insufficient knowledge of the highly specific yet diverse
requirements of popular musical choreography. And choreographic steps are *not* written down in order to pass them on to
future generations of choreographers, although musical notes

1

and stage directions are always available to succeeding generations of music directors and play directors. Where can someone thrust into this position of responsibility quickly learn what experience alone can teach?

Unfortunately, musical theater books to date have mostly been of an analytical or historical nature, and books published on choreography have dealt exclusively with classical ballet or modern dance. Therefore, few have provided concrete advice on the undertaking of a popular music production. The material presented here serves as a link between the two categories of musical theater and choreography. With enough texts explaining the mechanics of movement, and choreography in general, already on the market, this is *not* a book on dance technique. Rather, it is a catalogue for understanding the principles and procedures of which the musical theater choreographer must be aware.

In my travels, working across the United States and internationally, I have seen the many conditions in which choreographers work, and I have heard many of the same questions arise from novices who do not have access to professional training or experience. My years in the New York arena have revealed that many choreographers do not have a clearly defined concept of their responsibilities, or a sense of direction in their work. Of course, solutions and steps for specific instances must remain dependent upon each choreographer's own problem-solving ability.

My goal in *Musical Theater Choreography* is to offer general approaches, starting points, considerations, and alternatives for dealing with common musical theater situations. Professionals as well as amateur choreographers can benefit from this systematized presentation of duties, as will dancers branching out into the world of choreographic direction. Additionally, other members of the production staff who read this book may influence their own achievements in new ways, or simply gain insight into the choreographic process for its own sake.

The art of choreography owes a great deal of its progress to the creativity and contributions of women. I would never want to be accused of underestimating the work of women in this field. However, in order to make the amount of writing more manageable for this book, I have chosen the traditional pronoun "he" when referring to choreographers, directors, musicians, actors, and actresses. Again, respect and admiration for our female artists is implied at all times in this work.

Ultimately, the message of this book is that of inspiration to the developing choreographer. Therefore, I hope that what you do after reading this book is *create*. For *your* stage, *your* dancers, *your* productions, *your* self!

1 THE ROLE OF THE CHOREOGRAPHER

The mounting of a musical comedy is always a complex undertaking because there are so many elements that must be coordinated. On a conceptual level, the style and the treatment of the production must be decided upon in terms of script interpretation, stage direction, music direction, choreography, casting, scenery, costumes, lighting, and props. On an organizational level, a cast must be chosen and taught, rehearsal time and space efficiently scheduled, technical crews gathered and assigned tasks, and provision made for the musical accompaniment. On a physical level, the technical materials and lighting instruments must be obtained, every prop, costume and set piece designed and constructed, and the rehearsals paced so that the scenes, songs, dances, and music can be effectively learned and polished.

If we consider that these are the general requirements for *any* musical comedy, it is clear that delegating tasks in these areas is essential. For this purpose, a "production staff" is assembled: director, music director, choreographer, stage manager, set designer, costume designer, lighting designer, and props person. This staff should share an image of the finished production; the blending of their contributions must reflect a clear, common goal.

This image is supplied by the director, who provides guidelines for the manner in which the musical will be

5

presented. It is to his concept that this collaboration of specialists will conform. However, our focus is on the choreographer: how he relates to the other members of the production staff, to the performing company, to the material to be created, and to himself as an artist.

The choreographer is, essentially, an expert on body movement. As such, he will put to use a broad range of abilities, including knowledge of various dance vocabularies, signals for expressing emotion or situation, how to execute athletic feats, and how to make effective use of numerous individuals on stage. He may play a variety of roles in the course of his work. He could be a director, using only movement to convey his message; a designer, shaping the lines of the body to create pictures and patterns; a musician, working within a musical structure to make his own statement; a psychologist, projecting how a character will behave in a given situation; a teacher, communicating his ideas to his performers; a theatrical technician, utilizing the lights, sets, costumes, and props to enhance his work; an interpreter, transforming the director's concept into reality; or an artist, representing the intentions of the show's original production staff through his own creativity.

The choreographer's primary function is defining and supplying the specialized movement needs of the entire project. Unlike rehearsals with the director and music director, choreographic rehearsals for dances and staging will consume a great amount of the cast's time.

Because each production staff member has his own contribution to make, it is important to understand how each department functions in relation to the choreographer, and how the choreographer's work is only one part of a larger process.

THE DIRECTOR

To the director, the choreographer serves artistically as expert, interpreter, collaborator, and consultant of movement. He translates certain visual aspects of the director's concept into physical realities, and assesses exactly what is needed in the earliest stages. Once the members of the production staff have read the script and score, meetings are held so that the director can explain how he wants to present the piece. The choreographer then creates his material to fit into and advance this centralized concept.

Musical staging is, briefly, movement performed during a song, as opposed to strict dance choreography, and can run the gamut from intimate solos and duets to full ensemble numbers. Depending upon the type of musical number and treatment of production, the director may choose to stage some or all of these episodes, leaving only the actual dances to the choreographer. At other times, the musical staging may be completely left up to the discretion of the choreographer. My experience advises that at least the larger or more active chorus numbers should be done by the choreographer to cement an overall style and pace in the production. This allows for the reappearance of certain gestures or dance combinations wisely placed throughout the show, making for continuity while avoiding a feeling of redundancy.

Continuity of visual vocabulary helps to establish the identity of a production as well as those of the performers; a sudden divergence of style only makes an audience uncomfortable. The effect can be similar to actors in a dialogue scene suddenly adopting and then dropping a foreign accent. For example, I once choreographed a summer stock production of *West Side Story* in which the director wanted to stage only the "Jet Song." Because we put the show together in just fifteen hours of rehearsal, neither of us had the chance to observe each other's work. Result? The Jets moved in one style during the opening "Prologue," changed to a totally different type of gesturing for the "Jet Song," and then resumed their "Prologue" mannerisms for the rest of the show.

Collaboration on the part of the director and the choreographer is vital to the beginnings and endings of musical numbers. This means knowing where the performers are and what they are doing at the commencement of the music as well as where they must end up for the scene to resume. The best productions are "seamless" in that you cannot tell where or when the authority for direction changed hands.

A good director understands and works within the context of the written material. He may alter external trappings through degrees of stylization, but he keeps the spirit and intent of the original work intact. For example, in *Oklahoma!*, Laurey's dream ballet follows a specific story line which is underscored by musical themes. The dream ballet advances the plot and mood of the show as the show's authors intended. In creating another production, it is important to reproduce this story line, using the music as a guide to arrive at the same place dramatically. The choreographic steps may not be original, but the content and structure should be.

Most directors respect these often-produced musicals and revive them as written. However, there are some who attempt to "save" these classics by restructuring important elements to suit the director's whim. I once worked with a director who wanted to cut most of the dances out of *Brigadoon* and then include a new ballet. Another director wanted to make massive cuts in the *Oklahoma!* dream ballet and completely rewrite the sequence. Of course, every production will not be a full-scale Broadway revival mounted by a staff faithfully re-creating the original. Therefore, a certain amount of adaptation will always be necessary. However, *what* you are presenting is and must be the original material. *How* you decide to present it is your artistic choice and personal contribution.

It is important that the director and the choreographer agree upon the boundaries of artistic authority. Even though the show may be patterned to the director's general scheme, the choreographer should still have a measure of artistic freedom within that framework. There *are* times when a director has definite ideas about how part or parts of a number should look in order to achieve a certain effect. Nonetheless, since both the director and the choreographer deal with visual aspects of the performances and share a responsibility for directing the cast, mutual respect and courtesy are important to maintain.

Sometimes directors do not seem to care about the musical numbers. Other directors may care too much, interfering with work, interrupting rehearsals, or changing steps and gestures without the choreographer's consultation or approval. As a result, any critical exchange between staff members should take place privately, in the form of either a three-minute "time out" during a rehearsal or a scheduled conference. An open discussion or conflict in front of the performers can only make one or both of the parties look bad and erode company respect.

These examples are not to suggest that all directors are a discourteous, untrustworthy lot. An organized director, prepared to go into rehearsal, articulate his concepts, and be appreciative of the contributions of others, is a joy to work with.

THE MUSIC DIRECTOR

The music director, naturally, serves as the authority on music for the production. As such, he is responsible for the faithful and accurate performance of the show's score, encompassing all the music that is heard. He must have the ability to coordinate the various musical elements, assess the requirements of the score, and determine the capabilities of the available talent. He teaches the principals and ensemble the melodies (pitches, timings, harmonies), lyrics (words, diction, phrasing), and dramatic dynamics. Not only does he rehearse the orchestra members who have been chosen, but he must find them as well. *And* he must supply pianists for the staging, choreographic, and vocal rehearsals, if he does not accompany them himself.

The music director should be prepared to answer all questions about the music. His fluency in the language makes him the interpreter and guide for the choreographer through the passages to be staged. Together, they examine the score, listening to a piano play-through, while following the structure in print. The music director must also be ready to suggest alterations to what is written, adapting material and finding solutions for restrictive production circumstances. For him as well as the choreographer, the music becomes a map to help plot the dramatic and emotional imagery.

SCENIC, COSTUME, AND LIGHTING DESIGNERS

The scenic, costume, and lighting designers combine their talents to give the show its singular look. The work of the play's director and choreographer, being of a physical, visual nature dealing with the placement and movement of the performers, will be directly affected by the staff's designs.

Each designer will take basic physical realities and transform them into the elements representing the world in which the show takes place. For example, a staircase can be constructed in any number of sizes, shapes, or paths. But what would be appropriate for a given instance?

As a group, the artistic designers must establish guidelines by which the plans will be drawn: degree and manner of stylization, specific historical vogue, linear qualities, and choices of colors, including shades and tones. Individually, they must also account for the execution of these plans in regard to budget, time, attainable materials, and complexity of construction. Do the sketches represent a realistic goal? Are the diagrams too elaborate for the particular production?

The *scenic designer* considers the bare set pieces and their placement as dictated by the script, assembles them into a complete picture, and embellishes them in accordance with the central treatment. To accomplish the set design goals, he may have to discuss in production meetings matters like these: Where do such items as doorways, windows, walls, staircases, fireplaces, hedges, trees, or fountains go? How much of the stage area may be filled? What are the special demands of the blocking? Is there an ensemble dance in the scene? How many of the set pieces must be "practical," that is, physically usable? How easily can the set be changed to the next in sequence?

The *costume designer* must know more than the time and place of the show to create a mode of dress. He will also have some questions to ask in preliminary meetings, such as: How realistic for the setting should the clothing be? How can characterizations be suggested in the individuality of the outfits? What movements will be performed during the wearing? How quickly will the costume changes need to be completed during the show?

The job of the *lighting designer* involves, at the very least, guaranteeing that the performers can be seen. The changes in lighting can support every fluctuation of mood. The lighting designer should take into consideration the appearance of the scenery; the colors being used in the sets and the costumes; the reflective properties of the materials; whether lighting alone will define the playing area, or whether there are surrounding set pieces; and which effects—shadows, silhouettes, angles, or highlighting—are being sought.

Consultations among these different designers are of utmost importance to ensure proper coordination of the total work. Each technical aspect of the play will affect another technical aspect. For example, the costumes, wigs, or hats have to be small enough to get through the doorways; lighting on the scrim has to provide the planned translucency; and the steps up to the platform have to be large enough for the footwear. I know of one local production where red, black, silver, and white had been chosen to be the exclusive colors. Each designer labored for months over his aspect of the show, and at the production meetings all agreed to the effectiveness of this scheme. Finally, the day came when the performers stood before the new sets in their costumes, and the shades of red did not match! The scenery's tint leaned toward a yellowish hue and the costumes' tint toward a blue one—a hideous combination. The lighting only accentuated the problem because it flattered one shade and clashed with the other.

THE STAGE MANAGER

Though not creatively involved in the making of the artistic decisions, the stage manager is the master organizer of the group. He makes sure that rehearsals stay on schedule, that the facilities needed are available, and that all required participants are present. He duly notes any technical innovations or questions that arise during the blocking practice and contacts the appropriate department. He alerts the cast as to when they are needed and where, what they need to be prepared to learn, what to have ready, and any change in schedule or conditions.

In the professional theater, responsibility for the quality of the production goes from the director to the stage manager on opening night. Carefully recording the blocking as well as all of the technical cues in his script, the stage manager is in charge of the show in performance: calling the technical cues, supervising the set changes, preparing entrances, and generally solving contingent problems.

In contrast, a local community production which plays for a limited engagement will usually have the director and the stage manager sharing duties even after opening night.

THE PROPS MANAGER

The person who assembles the props for the show must have constant communication with the play's director, scenic designer, and, sometimes, the choreographer. Some hand props, as opposed to large set pieces or furniture, serve particular functions in the scenes and numbers in which they appear. Is a given object the size, weight, shape, and style that the director has in mind? For the scenic designer, does this item fit into the design scheme of the setting in which it is to be used? All props must agree with the design concepts of the production. If props are to be involved in the choreography, facsimiles will have to be available for the choreographer's experimentation and for use by the performers in rehearsal.

THE CHOREOGRAPHER

The choreographer is in a unique situation. While the director has the existing dialogue to represent, the music director has the established score to reproduce, and the designers have their physical requirements and periods of style predetermined, the choreographer is merely given an indication of the content which his work is to convey. Initially, he must go through the process of coordinating the script and score, hear the music to correlate its elements with the dramatic lines, and then make up his choreographic subject matter. He embarks on his task with only the given situation of the piece, the music, his imagination, and his vocabulary of movement. The choreographer must figure out the progressions in his segments and write a "script" out of his own steps—in essence, he must create a unique language of movement.

Steps in themselves only tell us counts, rhythms, and movements. Dancing must represent externalized dramatic emotion as well. A sleepwalker may smile because of a wonderful dream, but all someone outside of the body can perceive is the smile, not the inner vision.

A dance in a musical most often comes from some motivation. The number is included to make a statement that advances the dramatic line or enhances audience interest. Even if a musical number is needed structurally, a dramatic justification must be found. The bottom line is that everyone seen on stage is an *actor*. In choreography, acting must be conveyed via the dance. As the choreographer builds his material—from a series of static poses, moving steps, and counted routines up through combinations performed to music—the dance will remain sterile unless the element of acting is brought into play to lend a specific energy and purpose.

The intent of a musical number has several dimensions. The choreographer must answer questions such as:

- What does the dance number as a whole contribute to the dramatic line of the play?

- What is transpiring within the dance number itself?

- What end result is the dance aiming for through its structure?

- What is the number's climax?

- What mood(s) pertain to which sections of the numbers?

- What intensities and dynamics apply to which steps and phrases?

- What feelings and actions do the steps display?

- How can the dancing be augmented by acting?

"Acting" and "performing" are two separate qualities, though the choreographer must draw upon both of them in his work. Acting is the expression of definite, identifiable emotions through exaggerated actions; the reasons for the behavior are dramatically known. Performing is a charismatic quality—an energized state or facade without specifically scripted motivation besides "selling" to the audience. Performing expresses energy or feeling without necessarily resting on a specific foundation or subtext.

Acting takes place within the "world of the show," whereas performing concerns personal reception by the audience. One can perform with or without an acting context, but acting will not be effective without some degree of performance. Acting takes place in a designed set of dramatic circumstances; performing is a general approach to displaying oneself.

Audience empathy is another choreographic consideration. While not many people get up and dance about something in their lives, everyone feels emotion. Sharing an emotion connects the audience and the stage. Steps that are performed for their own sake can be technically brilliant yet dull. But steps that are *acted*, displaying human elements of feeling, will carry the audience to the purpose of the piece. The viewers will share whatever the performer is experiencing—tenderness, loneliness, or silliness—if the steps are appropriate, and if emotion brings color and depth to their delivery.

An audience will always accept simplistic choreography of otherwise meaningless steps as long as there is valid motivation for the dance and a committed delivery. Dance combinations executed without feeling may garner appreciation, but not caring or involvement from the audience. Therefore, it is vital for the dancers to fully understand what they are supposed to be conveying.

The choreographer must formulate the proper combinations for the dancers' abilities and potentials, helping them to look their best. No one wants to be displayed struggling to be adequate. Demanding the most growth and refinement possible, the choreographer should avoid pushing the performers beyond their physical and mental limits during a given rehearsal. He must consult with the music director to ensure that the choreographic demands are physically possible in conjunction with the vocal requirements of the score. Will there be enough energy and breath to do it all? What actions and activity precede and follow the complete number?

The challenge of choreography lies in making the production work best under the *given* circumstances. In a professional situation today, although one is dealing with trained, experienced performers, preparation is limited to a few hurried days or weeks to cut rehearsal costs and bring in profit as soon as possible. In the amateur case, a rehearsal period may span months, but every moment will be utilized teaching, repeating, building speed, and cleaning steps because of the performers' lack of background. Most of the time, the choreographer will have to cut out segments of choreographic material in order to spend more time in perfecting the performance.

Because the potential of the choreographer's work will be determined by the possibilities and restrictions of the surrounding physical realities, he must be absolutely certain of conditions such as space availability, set pieces, costumes, lighting, and props. And, often enough, some facet of these very elements will spark additional inspiration as the work progresses.

The choreographer is the staff member who will spend the majority of the time working with the performers, not only as a group, but on a one-to-one basis: teaching, correcting, and interacting. Just as every person is seen in the dance, so every person warrants choreographic attention. Consequently, the choreographer is second only to the play's director in the staff-company relationship.

Everyone enters the first rehearsal with a certain amount of excitement and apprehension. In a theatrical situation, where one is on display for peers in rehearsal and an audience later, the pressure can be devastating. In a vocal chorus, mistakes are impossible for the audience to identify: if an actor cannot sing, he can fake it by moving his lips and producing no sound, yet remain undetected. As soon as someone embarks in a choreographic pattern, however, he is totally exposed. In fact, instead of being able to conceal himself in a crowd, the more people involved, the more precise are the demands. If an error occurs, it draws attention to itself. There is an old saying that if there are sixteen dancers on stage and one of them is wrong, who will the audience watch? The other fifteen might as well go home.

Finally, the choreographer must fulfill the most basic responsibility of any theatrical enterprise: giving the audience

what it wants to see while trying to surpass what is antici-
pated. If the offering does not at least communicate and entertain, what is it for? The choreographer must work with the
production staff to move the audience to feel the right emotion
at the right time. As the show spins a thread of transitory
feelings through its scenes, songs, and dances, it should maneuver the sympathies of the audience without drawing attention to its methods. If the choreographer produces work
which only he and his coworkers comprehend, but which fails
to garner audience acceptance, then the show represents a
lack of communication, and the artist has succeeded only in
entertaining himself.

RESEARCHING THE ORIGINAL PRODUCTION

Any musical which is being revived is selected for one reason
above all others: the play has been a success in the past. For
the choreographer to give a valid foundation to his own version, research on the original production is of utmost importance. There are three main areas of research to pursue—
history, treatment, and response.

Historical questions to be asked include the following:
Was the show derived from another format (novel, play, film)?
What was its original intent? How did the intent change in the
transition? What was its relevance to current events at the
time? Does it reflect contemporary production styles? What
evolution did the original go through that culminated in the
final version we know today?

Treatment (manner of style and production) questions include: How was the material presented? Beyond the actual
script and score, how were the ideas conveyed visually and
physically? Are videotapes of earlier productions of a show
available?

Response questions include: What was the public and critical reception to the original? Where does the show stand in
the chronology of musical theater in terms of innovation, progression, and contribution? What is it famous *for*?

Understanding how and why something worked is different from blindly and mechanically performing a show

exactly as the original was done. Still, there is a mystique surrounding the original production, as though it was and remains the only True Way to present the piece.

What we see in the various elements of the first production is each staff member's contribution to his field. We are actually witnessing the producer's selection of artistic personnel. Who is to say that another artist's work would not have been just as effective or even better suited for the project? In some cases, additional specialists, usually uncredited, have been brought in to "doctor" and rescue an ailing endeavor, so the amount of work by the credited artist is actually unknown.

The original production also represents the opinions of the staff members at the time of the opening performance. Would any of them hold exactly the same interpretation if presented with the material at another time in his career, or under different conditions?

Even when faithful Broadway revivals are attempted, there can be problems. Every theater and stage is unique in its capabilities. Obviously, the original was geared for a fully-equipped Broadway house, chosen because of its design features, and the production schemes were adapted to suit the theater.

In order to plan *your* production, you have to consider the following: Will the current production be in a local professional theater, school, or gymnasium? On what kind of stage: proscenium, three-quarter thrust, or in the round? How large will be the stage be? Is there wing space? Is there a full or partial loft? What notable effects does the script require? How will the effects be adapted to your space? How will sets, costumes, lighting, and props be used?

In terms of casting, the original production had all of the trained professional performers in New York from whom to choose; however, amateur groups have more difficulty in finding the appropriate talent. The final version of the musical was formulated around the abilities of the participating performers, and in a sense was custom-made: whichever key was best for the soloist at the time was written in the score, thereby cementing a prerequisite for future casting of that part.

Of course, the same show's choreographer did much the same by assigning dance specialties to highlight a performer's gifts. But the choreographer's work, unlike the musical material, was not recorded and published. Consequently, the choreographer's contribution is often composed afresh.

Today, as never before, it is possible to obtain videocassettes and film versions of most popular musicals, and from them learn steps and copy choreography. These tapes are valuable as educational resources for the aspiring choreographer, but problems arise when they are used as the basis for a new production. Are the local dancers capable of executing the technically advanced materials? If the original staging is used, the performers end up cheated of compositions tailormade for their level, and may look like they are struggling beyond their abilities. And the choreographer would be cheating himself of an opportunity for practical experience and artistic growth.

2 CHOREOGRAPHIC CLUES IN THE SCRIPT AND SCORE

There are two primary sources for the content of musical dance: the script and the score. The kind of information to be gathered from each differs in point of reference and application, but both can combine to render a practical framework for the pieces. The script will provide a general outline, while the score will designate specifics coordinating the action with the music.

The script indicates when the dances occur. Sometimes a rough description is supplied, such as what is to take place during a dance—a brief scenario or dramatic theme to be followed, a mood to be set, or combinations of the two. These hints are usually no longer than a phrase like "They dance." The printed matter is only concerned with the elements which advance the plot for the reader. Once the script has stated that a dance does take place, the choreographer must derive the content of the dance from the text, either directly or indirectly.

The score reveals much about the intended staging of the numbers, functioning as a blueprint of the progressions to which the choreographer adds his own accents and structure. While the script will tell when a dance occurs and what it is about, the score will indicate how these ends are to be accomplished. What does the music sound like? What emotions and suggestions of movement are conveyed? Sometimes there are verbal descriptions of actions posted above correlating passages in the music, so that the feelings evoked by the sound of those phrases are linked to their visual representation.

THE SCRIPT

The script usually refers to incidents included in the dance in terms of stage directions which describe the actions and explain the dramatic goings-on. If there is an extended ballet sequence composed of distinct episodes, there is a good chance that the script will summarize it incident by incident if it is important to the overall plot of the show, especially if there is vocal support involved. Of course, there can be some confusion, because the lyrics themselves do not explain how the dancers dance.

For example, in the episode from *Guys and Dolls* when Sky and Sarah visit Havana, the dance and mime segments are pierced with occasional lines of dialogue from the two leads, although Sky and Sarah do not become dance figures or absorbed into the surrounding dance. If these scattered statements were written in the script without any indication of the concurrent and following dance activity, the reader would still be able to interpret the sightseeing and drinking. However, not only would the characterization be sorely underdeveloped, but, without the dance action, the subsequent change in Sarah's behavior, the resulting brawl, and the acceleration of the pacing into the following song would all be missing.

Or in *Carousel*, when the ballet on the beach is interrupted with speech, could the scene be accurately approached in terms of the dialogue alone? Imagine that this is all that is offered:

ACT II   Scene 4

(On a beach. Fifteen years later. Louise is dancing on the beach. Enter Mr. Snow's Daughter.)

Miss Snow: My father bought me my pretty dress.

Louise: My father would have bought me a pretty dress, too. He was a barker on a carousel.

Miss Snow: Your father was a thief.

(Louise chases her off.)

Louise: I hate you—I hate all of you.

Here, the dialogue conveys an extremely rudimentary sense of what is going on. We understand Louise's situation in the community, but virtually no indication is given of the ballet that, in its fully developed form, covers eighteen pages of music.

If the only information supplied is that "there *is* a dance," the lack of further commentary forces the choreographer to explore neighboring material in the script to deduce what is supposed to transpire. How does the dance fit in to the plot? What plotted elements can be incorporated to the segment's dance movements?

Take the "Crapshooters' Dance" from *Guys and Dolls.* The script gives us no indication that any specific actions are to occur. It tells us where people are at the beginning of the number, and the reference says, "When the dance is finished. . . ." Obviously, the dance should exhibit stylized forms of men shooting craps, but *what* is expected for 260 bars of music? When we look at the dialogue at the top of the following scene, however, we find the characters discussing Big Jule's mammoth losses incurred during the preceding twenty-four-hour game. Aha! This tells us what the dance is supposed to illustrate—the men gambling with Big Jule, who repeatedly loses.

A major consideration for the development of any choreographic dance is the copy of the script one is reading. Although you may think that all scripts are the same, they are not. While most scripts purport to include a complete listing of all the lines of both dialogue and lyrics, the amount of production information and explanation varies widely from script to script. Basically, musical scripts come in four types: working libretto, booklet/typed copy, published libretto, and sides.

The *working libretto* is by far the most complete form of script—almost too complete. It is a written record preserving the original production in print. Besides featuring every bit of principal directorial blocking, it may include a lighting plot, spot cues, wardrobe assignments for every member of the company, complete prop lists with their replacements, and even ideal time limits for each scene. Yet even in this comprehensive treatment, the dances will be dismissed for the most part with something like "The girls dance to the reprise" ("Many a New Day" in *Oklahoma!*).

The *booklet* or *typed copy* is the form in which most rented scripts will appear. Again, there is great detail about some aspects of the production, yet almost no detail about other aspects. There are no hard and fast rules about which dance numbers will be summarized and which will not. The booklet for *On the Town* illustrates this type of problem. The actions leading into the dance accompanying the song "Lonely Town" are clearly scripted, and the major ballet of the second act, "Dream Coney Island," is outlined in definite imagery. Yet the climax and finale of the entire first act is reduced to the directions that the Nedick's stand disappears and the Times Square ballet begins. There is no hint as to what is to be done with the following nineteen pages of complex ballet music.

The third format is called the *published libretto* or published script. These are the hardbound, paperback, and anthology copies sold on the commercial market. While they are not really printed for use in production, they serve people who want to study the text or relive the show through reading. Published librettos used to be the only versions of the script which included pictures of the original production, a practice since discontinued. They are adequate enough for the actor to use for learning his lines and making his notes, but, except for the older copies with photos, are next to useless to the creative staff. These books must also be checked for discrepancies, since their content is not always identical with the production version. The published script of *Man of La Mancha*, for example, lacks the scene in the stable when Aldonza talks to the animals, and her song, "What Does He Want of Me?". The anthology copy of *Carousel* includes a second Heavenly Friend who was later combined with the first to make a single character.

The final script format is *sides*. A side consists of incomplete parts of a script, either as an individual actor's lines, typed with their preceding cues and bound as a little script of its own, or as isolated pages of scenes. The director alone receives a complete script. The faults of this system are numerous, and there are few advantages in it for the performing company. There is the financial benefit: using sides is cheaper because the companies that rent out these shows do not have to reprint the entire play. Unfortunately, the cast members simply do not know what is going on from scene to scene and from number to number. They cannot even read to find out what the show is about! Every time I have had to work with this annoying system, I have photocopied the director's copy of the script so all involved were equipped with the same material. The expense was minor compared to the inconvenience and confusion of a piecemeal approach.

THE SCORE

Choreographic markings in the score are more specific than those in the script. In the score they are written over exact phrases of music to denote what action took place at that moment in the original production. Consider that for the original production, the music was molded to augment the choreography and the choreography was tempered to meld with the music.

Rarely do the choreographic labels refer to exact steps, so the markings do not appear copiously. Pieces consisting of only dance with no dramatic dialogue will be devoid of these guidelines at all. Here, too, there are no hard and fast rules. Some scores are totally lacking any such help, while others offer more details. General descriptions similar to those in the script, like these for *Carousel*'s "June Dance," are occasionally found: "The girls dance with abandon and convey to the audience the sentiment associated with the month of June." Most frequently, the scores will signify entrances and exits. For example, the "Havana" sequence in *Guys and Dolls* includes a bit of sightseeing, four nightclubs, and extended mime and fight segments—yet the score only indicates dialogue, as well as the entrances and exits of the principals and the native "Cubanos." One must derive the rest of the choreographic action from the script, or freely invent dance material.

The amount of guidance in the score varies greatly from show to show. The "Prologue" in the score of *West Side Story* lists the entrances and exits of the Jets and the Sharks, and says that two Jets taunt Bernardo, a Shark trips a Jet, and Bernardo pierces A-rab's ear. After that information, the choreographer is on his own, though it is clear that there should be high-energy action as all hell breaks loose for 103 measures of music. The score of *The Music Man* extends no choreographic help at all, despite lengthy segments that present music, lyrics, and necessary dialogue. "The Small House of Uncle Thomas" ballet from *The King and I* is a treasure trove of material—not only are all the movements described in the accompanying working libretto's narration, but the summaries in the script and the score fully explain the proceedings.

There are times when plot, music, and staging can join simultaneously to create a moment pivotal to the entire show, such as the deaths of Riff and Bernardo in the "Rumble" of *West Side Story*. The score itself has the exact musical notes meant to coordinate with the opening of the knives and Tony's killing of Bernardo marked with arrows, so that both the music director and the actors know exactly when these actions are supposed to occur.

To give an example of notations which are a real gift to the choreographer, let us look again at the ballet on the beach from *Carousel*. Here, every important incident and development is duly noted in the score above the corresponding measures of music:

> The daughter, Louise, is discovered standing alone on a beach in full morning light. She runs and leaps and tumbles in animal joy. She turns a somersault and lies down on the sand to stare at the sky. Two ragged urchins come in leap-frogging. She joins them in their rough play. Mr. Snow enters followed by six little Snows in Sunday hats in single file. They stop in amazement to see the boisterous roughhousing of Louise and her companions. Mr. Snow strongly disapproves. Louise asks them to play with her. They snub her and leave. A younger Miss Snow lags behind out of curiosity. She examines Louise's poor dress and bare feet with unfriendly dislike. Miss Snow is stuck up. The children speak:

Miss Snow: My father bought me my pretty dress.

Louise: My father would have bought me a pretty dress, too. He was a barker on a carousel.

Miss Snow: Your father was a thief.

Louise chases her in a rage and steals her fancy hat. The boys approve. A carnival troupe comes in, headed by a young man who is like what Louise believes her father to have been. She is enchanted and excited by their costumes. She snatches the gold parasol of the leading acrobatic lady. The carnival people perform a brutal and frenetic waltz. The acrobatic lady sees Louise holding the stolen parasol and demands it back. The young man and Louise meet face to face. He tells her not to mind and winks at her. The carnival people exit. Louise is alone on the beach with the young man who has waited behind. He makes love to her. In spite of herself she is drawn to him. He grows frightened at her intensity. Realizing she is only a child he leaves her and goes away. She feels humiliated and ashamed. She weeps. A children's party comes in dancing a polonaise. She tries to join them but is constantly pushed out. Louise tries to play by herself outside of the party. Her heart breaks. Miss Snow makes fun of her. All the children begin to mock. Louise turns on them in desperation. They are frightened by her fury.

Louise (she whispers): I hate you! I hate all of you!

The children continue dancing oblivious to her agony. She is an outcast.

This would certainly answer any questions about what is supposed to occur. Yet as complete as this breakdown seems, even more surprising is the summary that appears in the script, which tells the same story in different images and details:

. . . Now a carnival troupe dances on. The ruffians are frightened by them. Failing to persuade Louise to run away with them, they leave her there. One of the carnival boys is the type Louise's father was when he was young. Of all this fascinating group, he interests her the most. After the others dance off, he returns to her for a flirtation. It is much more then this for Louise. It is a first experience, overwhelmingly beautiful, painful and passionate. He leaves her abruptly. She's too young. Thwarted, humiliated, she weeps alone . . .

Where is the lady acrobat and her parasol? Do we learn of the reactions of the two urchin-ruffians other than how and when they exit? Compare the score's description of this episode with the script's summary of the same incident. The former is externally-oriented, telling us what is happening visually on stage, while the latter is a bit more lush in its adjectives and motivations, offering the choreographer and dancers a breadth of creative possibilities.

Scripts and scores that have a bountiful quantity of information to use as a springboard for choreographic work are exceedingly and, sadly, rare. The choreographer is too often stymied by the necessity of having to invent his own dramatic *content* in addition to dance movements. When adequately supplied, however, choreographic notations in the script, combined with markings in the score, can give a good picture of the purpose and feeling of the piece and act as a definite starting point toward creating variations on the original themes.

In comparing the two systems of script and score, the choreographer must always be aware of possible discrepancies. The notations of the "Miss Turnstiles" ballet from *On the Town* are typical: the script gives a chronological run-down of the dialogue as it is interspersed with the action and music. The score indicates the choreographic entrance of each section and where the music serves as an underscoring for the announcer's speeches. Yet a vocal lyric of the announcer's in the script does *not* appear in the score, and a choral number in the vocal music books is in neither the conductor's score nor the script! In such a case, the creative staff must decide which version is best suited for their own production, and make sure that the scripts and scores are coordinated properly.

3 UNDERSTANDING
THE SCORE

The content of the musical is preserved in its printed script and score. The ability to read the language of the script, transforming the letters on the page into ideas and speech, is fundamental in comprehending the piece. However, when a score is played aloud, the listener needs no familiarity with its written language to feel the composer's intentions. The music can be enjoyed divorced from any academic knowledge of its structure.

Like the script, the score represents a series of progressive ideas. Hearing music is as transitory an act as is viewing a play: when either performance is finished, it is gone in the air. Existing afterward only as a memory, the content can be remembered generally, but the mercurial nature of recollection proves to be a faulty tool when intricate retrospect is required.

The reason that the choreographer must have musical expertise is that he is not a casual listener. He uses the music as one of the foundations of his creative work. As the choreographer follows along in a score and hears the music being played, he should be able to recognize certain notes, melodic lines, backgrounds, and exact phrases. There are tricks to this general understanding, but elementary knowledge of the musical language and its symbols is necessary for establishing points of reference. At the very least, the choreographer should not have to say to his pianist, "I'm not sure. What's that note near the top with the line running through it?" Much of the process of "following along" merely requires common sense. If the choreographer is by nature musically inclined, he will be surprised at how much music he already knows.

What *is* the score? The score is the total reducing to print of the music in a production, whether in a fully orchestrated arrangement or reduced to a solo piano version. A solo pianist, having ten fingers, can play up to ten notes at a given time, thus being able to reproduce the equivalent musical structure of ten instruments. Therefore, the piano reduction can duplicate or indicate the musical structure as will be used in orchestral performance, though in terms of piano sound.

TYPES OF MUSIC IN THE SCORE

To the choreographer, there are five basic classifications of music found in the score, as dictated by function: introductory/transitional, underscoring, songs, dance music, and overtures/*entr'actes*.

Introductory/Transitional Music

Introductory/transitional music initiates a piece or forms the bridge from one segment of the music to another. It introduces the material to the audience—establishing or shifting key signatures, time signature, tempo, or style—or changes the prevailing mood of the upcoming dance number of a scene. It is preparatory in nature and function, helping the audience shift gears for what is to come. This music can consist of an extended passage, a brief statement, or a repeated vamp (a musical idea, played in succession as many times as necessary to fill a gap in action). One might say that this type of music is *always* transitional, as it sets the atmosphere for the arrival of a new piece, whether making the transition from dialogue to musical statement, or from one musical statement to another—song to song, song to dance, underscoring to song/dance, from theme to theme, and so on. Such music will frequently require no specific staging, as when it is used to initiate the expansion of a musical number, as when a song enlarges into a choreographed ensemble. Its duration is designed to give the players time to set up the stage (moving furniture, changing starting places, or setting props to be used).

Underscoring Music

Underscoring music supports and adds dramatic background to scenic dialogue or action. It can be closely related to introductory passages, depending upon its length and use, such as when it is played under a scene and leads directly into a song or dance.

Effectively used, instrumental underscoring can unify the production by restating musical themes at appropriate times so that: (1) songs and dances do not stand as islands or intrusions in the flow of dramatic action, (2) a character becomes more closely identified with his or her theme, and (3) melodies can be applied dramatically to the scenes. Underscoring also achieves continuity in the production by linking musical statements, instead of breaking the mood each time a musical statement ends. An effective underscoring is displayed in the "If I Loved You" scene in *Carousel*, where underscored dialogue is frequently interspersed with blocks of sung lyric.

Because underscoring is used to accent action and provide undercurrent, it should not draw attention to its own presence. In its most common application, underscoring will utilize a theme, or variations on a theme, already heard (usually in the songs) and easily recognizable to the audience. This type of underscoring can often refer to a particular character as well as a song associated with that character. When the song "Something Wonderful" is used for underscoring in the latter part and the finale of *The King and I*, it is not identified with Lady Thiang, the character who first introduced the song and sang its reprise. Instead, it is identified with the king, the subject of the piece. The use of the cha-cha version of the song "Maria" in the second Bridal Shop scene in *West Side Story* recalls the circumstance of Tony and Maria's first meeting by recreating their initial music. The perkiness of "I'm in Love with a Wonderful Guy" is played instrumentally for both contrast and reminder when Nellie is informed that Emile is out on a dangerous mission in *South Pacific*.

Though stage actions and dialogue generally coincide with the underscoring, there is no specific choreographic structure to such music. The underscoring most often serves as background to natural action, rather than support for dance.

Songs

Songs, combining lyrics and melody, are in the foreground of the score, and are sung by one or more of the performers. Most of the standard songs have been written in 2/4, 3/4, 4/4, or 6/8 time, indicating beat patterns of two, three, four, or six to the measure.

Songs constructed in 2/4 or 4/4 time are built in "blocks" of four sets of eight-count lines equalling 32 beats. In a simplified example, count from one to eight four times in a row, keeping a steady beat. Your count now equals the time value of one block of music.

The framework is one of structure-within-a-structure. Once the system of "blocks" of music, as described above in the four-times-eight example, is established, we must explore *how* these blocks are used.

What developed in the musical theater was "verse-refrain" formats for most tunes that housed an "A-A-B-A" sequence of melodies. In the "A-A-B-A" construction, the melodic themes are introduced as follows:

1. Melody "A" is heard first as the primary theme

2. Melody "A" is repeated, now with different lyrics

3. A new melody, "B," is introduced, for 16 or 32 beats

4. Melody "A" is restated, again with new lyrics

Melody "B" is not a variation of "A"; it serves primarily to provide contrast to "A." Although there may be an abrupt break from "A" into the opening of "B" as a new idea, still, when "B" ends, there must be a feeling and need for the restoration of "A." Of course, the song may have additional melodies such as "C" and "D," but they work into or around the primary "A-A-B-A" pattern.

Lyrics	Counts
Luck be a lady tonight,	(8)
(A) Luck be a lady tonight,	(8)
Luck, if you've ever been a lady to begin with,	(8)
Luck be a lady tonight.	(8)
Luck let a gentleman see	(8)
How nice a dame you can be,	(8)
(A) I know the way you've treated other guys you've	
been with,	(8)
Luck be a lady with me.	(8)
A lady doesn't leave her escort, it isn't	(8)
(B) Fair, it isn't nice,	(8)
A lady doesn't wander all over the room	(8)
And blow on some other guys dice.	(8)
So let's keep the party polite,	(8)
(A) Never get out of my sight,	(8)
Stick with me baby, I'm the fellow you came with	(8)
Luck be a lady tonight.	(8)

In this example, the entire "A-A-B-A" framework comprises what may be called the *refrain*, which serves the purpose of providing the primary musical and dramatic statement of the song. It also tends to be the most recognizable and popular part, and is the section from which the song title is often drawn.

The *verse* and *refrain*, like the "A" and "B" melodies, are not necessarily variations of each other. They are different melodic ideas that work together to provide the piece's structure. The ending of one, which in most cases is the verse, calls for the return of the other continually, allowing for alternating use with different sets of lyrics. A common basic pattern is as follows:

1. Verse

2. Refrain: Melody A
             Melody A
             Melody B
             Melody A

3. Verse

4. Refrain: A-A-B-A

The "A-A-B-A" system was most often employed in popular songs before the advent of the modern musical comedy, and earlier shows reflect this influence.

The pursuit of novelty and the tailoring of material to suit dramatic circumstances led to new alignments of the basic structural parts. For example, in most musicals the verse is heard only once in an introductory capacity, serving as a bridge from the dialogue, stating the scripted premise, and setting up the situation and opinion on which the refrain will elaborate. Often both the verse and refrain will be played through only once each for the complete statement. The possibilities for verse-refrain combinations are endless, and examples of their diversity can be found in every musical produced.

Songs written in 3/4 time can also use a verse-refrain structure. When there are sections of a song in varying time length, the choreographer must still break the song down into a block system of eight-measure phrases or multiples thereof. The choreographer will find that variations abound. The "A-A-B-A" format can be used here as well in analyzing the structure of a song. In "Try to Remember" from *The Fantasticks*, the format runs the full pattern for the refrain, but contains no verse. *Brigadoon*'s "Come to Me, Bend to Me" demonstrates verse-refrain-verse-refrain, but contains no "B" melody in the refrain. Thus, the format is read as verse-"A"-verse-"A." The verse contains only eight measures, while the "A" melody has sixteen measures. Again, the choreographer works in multiples of eight beats.

Dance Music

Dance music is one of the choreographer's major concerns; here we are dealing with it solely as part of an overall score. Dances occur in two basic contexts: as song accompaniment, and as "free-standing" performance pieces. Certain music in the score—as with most scores by Leonard Bernstein, for example—can be written exclusively for dance numbers. Dance music frequently draws on song themes, especially if the dance supports adjacent vocal work. The dance music can suggest the melody line, recall it, or repeat it exactly.

Overtures/*Entr'actes*

The overture serves as the audience's initiation to the presentation, the portal through which they enter the "world of the show." An overture usually consists of an instrumental medley of the various songs, themes, and styles to be used in the performance to follow. As such, it receives no choreographic treatment. The overture helps the audience remove themselves from reality and obtain the desired mood for the show's opening. The *entr'acte* is an abbreviated overture that performs a similar function. It helps the audience become re-involved in the tone and plot of the action after they return from intermission.

Sometimes the overture is accompanied by action that is a prelude to the dramatic structure of the production. The prologue in *West Side Story,* for example, consists of choreography, while the prologue in *Carousel* is an underscored mimed ensemble dramatic scene, coordinated with themes in the music. Both *The Fantasticks* and *Carnival* greet their audiences with performers preparing for the presentation. Though these latter two openings do not contain incidents vital to the plot, they expose the viewers to introductory images, acclimating them to the world of the show. When an overture is used in this way, the medley format is often abandoned in favor of an original piece of music, as with *The Fantasticks* and *Carnival.*

Other Types of Music

There are additional types of music contained in a score; some of this music will require choreographic treatment, and some will not. For example, *set change music,* usually played in the dark, will either reprise a dominant theme, supply a mood transition from one scene to the opening of the next scene, or set the tone for the upcoming action. Normally, these pieces are listed in a score's table of contents as "Change of Scene."

A *playoff* is a separate piece of music used after a dance number has been completed to provide the transition back into dramatic action, smoothing the way for continuity. This type of music is used primarily when a large number has ended with a tableau, where all actors on stage freeze. The playoff allows time for the stage action to resume, and any amount of stage business can take place—the chorus can exit or return to places, characters can enter, and props can be taken away. It is timed to take place after the crest of the applause from the preceding number has been reached, and its beginning is used as the cue for the return to action. Musically speaking, the playoff can repeat the prominent melody or theme of the number it follows, or it can be merely an appropriate vamp to sustain the desired mood. Another name for the playoff is the *tag*, which serves the same supplementary function.

Other bits of music are often heard throughout productions to provide undercurrent or mood. In various scores, these snatches of melody are referred to in different terms. They may be called "incidentals," "underscoring," or may have specific titles according to their application, such as "opening of scene" and "closing of scene."

MUSIC IN PERFORMANCE

How will the music *sound* during the running of the show? *Hearing* the music—as opposed to seeing it in the score—is crucial to the creation of the choreography. Too often, the novice choreographer hears the full orchestration for the first time too late in the game, during the assembling of production elements, and laments, "If I had known the music was going to sound like *this*, I would have used it differently!" Listening to the total rendition is usually impossible during the primary creative period in the amateur situation, since the musicians themselves have not yet learned to play it, and, in a professional production, because the musicians have not yet been hired. The music director and the choreographer should meet frequently in these early stages to ensure high quality in the final results.

The original cast recording of the musical, since it is made with a complete orchestra, can offer a sample of the sound of the whole show. Yet these recordings provide a better glimpse of the songs than the dances: the show's dance music is frequently not even on the album. The choreographer should be aware that any dance music that does make it onto the recording is sometimes speeded up in order to save time for other material.

How will the score in your production be represented? Some performances are played with solo piano, just as in the rehearsal. Percussion would be the next most important addition to an amateur production's ensemble, followed by a bass part. The combination of these three types of musical instruments constitute a basic rhythm section. Key solo instruments can then be added, culminating, of course, in a full orchestra. The assumption here is that the musical source is live.

On occasion, taped music can be used, though an extremely efficient method of cueing must be available. The reason is that there is a considerable amount of start-and-stop music intermixed with the dialogue and scoring.

We will look closely at the requirements of the two major types of musical accompaniment for a performance: the live orchestra and taped material.

The Live Orchestra

The great advantage to working with live music is that the music director can rewrite or reorchestrate around any choreographic ideas. However, time must be allowed for any new arrangements to be written and for the musicians to learn them. The choreographer must know what he needs as early as possible so that the orchestra members do not waste their valuable time rehearsing material which will not be used or become drastically altered. Changes are to be minimized the further into the rehearsal schedule everyone works.

To the novice onstage performer, the full orchestra represents a potentially jarring adjustment from rehearsing, say, with a pianist. With the orchestra, numbers cannot be readily stopped and begun; tempos can vary, and may not be discussed until after the run-through. The melody, to which the dancer is used to counting, is suddenly obscured by the instrumentation. An interesting phenomenon occurs onstage which the choreographer should call to the dancers' attention: when one is dancing downstage in front of a live orchestra which stretches along the edge of an unmonitored stage (without speakers to help the performers hear the total sound), those onstage can *only* hear the section of the orchestra next to which they are dancing.

The Piano Score versus the Orchestral Score

There is a difference in the dramatic quality of the music from piano reduction to full orchestration. *Carousel* presents some good illustrations. The piano version of the "Hornpipe Dance" becomes suspiciously redundant, certainly not revealing the instrumentation that will bring the music to life. The rolling, tinkling arpeggios that open the ballet in the second act do not convey in rehearsal the power of the brass and percussion which will play that same passage in the performance. And the "June Dance" has a briskness in its piano form which does not extend to its orchestration.

    The choreographer must study and compare the piano score to the orchestral score with the music director to find any disparities between the two. By understanding the differences, the choreographer can head off any later surprises, and ensure consistency in the numbering of the measures. He should make notes in his piano score of any instrumentation indications, showing which sections of the orchestra will be playing predominantly during which portions of the music. In the piano reduction, the same melodic theme played in repetition can sound monotonous. With the orchestration supplied, the listener will discover that the strings play the theme once, the theme is repeated, possibly as a flute solo, and the entire brass section may handle the theme the third time around. The use of these various sections of the orchestra offers a great variation of mood and tone. Such reshapings of the basic melodic material are what the choreographer must find and develop. Any alternative version that deviates from the straight delivery should be sought out. In the end, the choreographer must have an accurate feeling of the mood the music will establish, for without this insight, his choreography will later prove to be inappropriate.

Tempos

Tempos (the speed of the music) should also be established early on. When the steps and routines are coming together in dance rehearsal, the choreographer should attend orchestra rehearsals to try out the dances, or pieces of the dances, himself. But even when doing so, the choreographer must allow for differences in technical ability between the dancers and himself. Will they be able to execute the material as cleanly as he can? If not, can the steps be done at a slower pace? Of course, some steps cannot be slowed down, such as turns, leaps, slides, and kicks. If the steps must be done at a greatly different rate of speed, the music director can adjust the tempo accordingly to change the entire pattern of step-to-count coordination.

The best approach is to refine the dance routines in such a way that there are two possible performance speeds: (1) an ideal speed, and (2) a slightly slower tempo. That small reduction in pace, while possibly shaving a thin edge off the excitement, can make all the difference between a fast, frantic mess and a cleanly, clearly performed pattern. The choreographer must make sure, however, that the combinations will work at *both* speeds.

Accents

Musical and dramatic accents can be a valuable means of highlighting an action in the staging of the dance. An accent supplies sound to a precise visual act. A slide whistle can be used for a humorous slip, slide, or pratfall. A cowbell can represent a kick in the pants. A bass drum is used when someone falls down or simply sits. An example of a dramatic accent is a gunshot represented by a rim shot. An event or sudden realization can be conveyed with a simple "ting" of a triangle. In an orchestral situation, any instrument, such as a trombone slide or a trumpet growl, can be used to provide an accent to an act.

Accents can also differentiate a musical phrase within a sequence. For example, if you have a thirty-two-count phrase (four sets of eight counts) and you choose to have the third set of eight accented with some additional sound, that phrase will convey a different mood because of the sound that is made. The variety of available accents can be placed anywhere: on the beat, off the beat, throughout a full set of eight counts, on the second beat of each set, and so on.

By relating his work to such accents, the choreographer can achieve a completely coordinated quality in his work. The instrumentalist and conductor must, of course, notate these additions in their scores. That way, every time the dancer wiggles her fanny in the choreography on counts one, two, and three, there is a cowbell clanging when desired on counts one, two, and three. Also, the choreographer must be able to communicate exactly what he wants and where the accent will appear in the music—another reason the choreographer should have basic music-reading skills.

Visual cues for musical accents should be avoided if possible. These cues would be freestanding events which, for various reasons, do not always occur in exactly the same way or with the same timing. Obviously, the musician will be reading his music and watching the conductor; he should not have to view the stage as well. It is always easier for the accent musician to coordinate action to rhythmic music than to try to anticipate an arbitrarily-timed movement.

Some accents are already supplied musically in the score, representing the original staging. These published accents are written into the show as part of the full orchestration, as an instrumental section, or as a solo instrument's part.

Sometimes one might hear grossly out-of-context sounds, such as moments, interruptions, or additions that do not go along with the flow of the music. When matched with the original action that they support, these musical places will become a valid statement of a special event.

The changing of some accents should not be confused with replotting or restructuring a piece. The choreographer should have the freedom to express whatever is valid to himself artistically with accents while working with certain "givens." Essential musical and dramatic coordination with accents must be preserved, such as the stabbings of Riff and Bernardo in *West Side Story*, where the music and the accents are written to climax at these peak moments.

Taped Music

While using prerecorded taped material in performance has its advantages, the liabilities of this method are much more numerous. On the "plus" side, a tape provides the full sound of the instrumental parts; the performance "unknowns" found in a live orchestra are not going to be there; the tape will sound exactly the same every time it is played; and assuming that a copy of the performance has been made available for rehearsals, the performers will not have to make the musical transition from practice music to stage music. Yet while the tape may be a perfect reproduction of the score, it may not suit the needs of the specific production. The use of taped material has the following drawbacks:

- The performers may not be mentally or technically capable of performing to the music. The tempo may be too fast for the speed, endurance, and breathing of the amateur dancers. On the other hand, the tempo may be too slow and can deprive the number of its vitality. A tape allows no conference with a conductor as to what tempo works best.

- The choreographer may want to delete or repeat certain sections of the music; doing so would be hard or impossible to manage with taped music.

- There may be too many technical roadblocks in the way of using the taped music of the original score and the current specific production. For example, the performance space may be so different from that of the original production that there is too much room, or too little time, to cross the stage or complete an action.

- If the performers make any mistakes during an actual performance, such as missing a cue, there is no one to help them cover up; the music rolls on.

- There is no visible conductor or music director to act as a unifying force for the people onstage to help with tempos and cues, unless someone is placed in the pit with headphones expressly for that purpose.

- Tapes require a flawless cueing system for the beginnings and endings of musical segments. The cueing can be a very tricky business, especially with musical comedy, where the numbers usually arise out of action or dialogue, and which may not start with predictable abruptness, as they would in a revue.

- Using taped music is especially difficult when the actors have to time dialogue or action with underscoring. A live conductor would adapt the length and speed of the music to the actor's progress through the material. With a tape, however, the actor must have one ear tuned to the timing of his accompaniment while playing the scene, to make certain he will finish with the music.

- Technical malfunctions with a tape are difficult, if not impossible, to hide. A back-up copy of the tape and an extra machine should be available. However, the action in progress is certain to halt, no matter what the accident—broken, twisted, or bunched-up tape, or a recorder malfunction.

If you are using taped music in performance, be prepared to use microphones extensively. When the taped material is being played over a public-address system or with a great volume increase, the difference in quality between the natural voice and artificial amplification will require mixing the voices to achieve the proper tonal balance.

4 WORKING WITH THE SCORE

I n musical comedy, the score is the foundation of the choreographer's work. It is more than a valuable tool for identifying specific passages, and more than the primary means of communicating with the musical director and the rehearsal pianist. The score serves another, equally vital function. The choreographer needs a method of writing down his work to keep his ideas in order, to coordinate his output with the music, and to safeguard against lapses of memory between his private time in formulation and his time spent at company rehearsals. The perfect vehicle for all these essential systems exists in the pages of the score. By effectively marking the score, the choreographer establishes the musical reference points that he will use to create the dance movements. Here is where the importance of the music director cannot be overstated. Not only can the music director answer questions about the material, but he can help the choreographer decipher parts of the score as well as offer alternatives and solutions.

THE COUNT SYSTEM

The first order of business in creating choreographic movements is listening to a play-through of the music and counting the phrasings to get a feel for the rhythms. The choreographer

41

will begin to construct a rudimentary framework in his mind by counting along as the music plays, measure by measure. Keep in mind: the beats in the music—that is, how many beats per measure and how the music is written—are different from the *counts* used in dance and choreography. Dances can be built around their own phrases, and there is not always a one-to-one correspondence between the structure of the dance and the structure of the music. For the choreographer, a phrase represents a complete musical statement to the ear, even though that phrase may actually be several bars of music.

Though most popular music is written in eight-count musical phrases, and counting in sets of eight seems to be the most comfortable basis for dancers to use, the idea is not for the choreographer to be limited solely to working in strict eight-count patterns, regardless of the course of the melody. The choreographer must feel how the phrasing of the melody lines begin and end, breaking up the music into natural divisions.

These phrases should sound like the beginnings and endings of musical thoughts. Sometimes, they will indeed be counted in strict eights. Sometimes, the phrasing and feel of the melody line will be erratic or inconsistent. And sometimes the music may not sound like it is being counted at all!

Which count system is to be used for dance? The time signature indicated for the piece may not seem appropriate for either the mood or the pacing of the physical activity. Does the written signature seem faster or slower than the dance steps can match? Upon hearing the music and counting along at a steady beat, the choreographer must discover the *dance tempo* and correlate it with the musical tempo as conducted from the score. A good example of this phrases/count correlation is the time signature of 6/8, which is most often counted as 2/4 dance tempo because a prominent two-beats-per-measure is how the rhythm is felt.

Initially, to find the number of beats in the phrases of a given piece, one can simply tap a finger on the beat as the music plays, allowing the number of taps per measure as prescribed in the time signature. These taps will later be filled in with numerical designations, determined according to the duration of the different phrases. Let us consider some examples of how count systems can be culled from various instances.

Eight-Count Phrases

In the most simplistic case, a number would be constructed exclusively in sets of eight-count phrases, like the "Farmer Dance" from *Oklahoma!*'s "The Farmer and the Cowman" number. Because the initial dance theme is actually a rendition of the song, the theme is also based on a thirty-two-count block system (four times eight counts). The "Farmer Dance" has the following structure:

Counts:	16	(2 × 8)	Introductory Vamp
	32	(4 × 8)	Theme A (repeat of song)
	32	(4 × 8)	Theme A
	16	(2 × 8)	Introductory Vamp
	32	(4 × 8)	Theme B
	32	(4 × 8)	Theme C
	32	(4 × 8)	Theme B
	32	(4 × 8)	Theme C
	16	(2 × 8)	Theme A
	24	(3 × 8)	Vamp
	16	(2 × 8)	Theme A

Four-Count Phrases

The first variation of this count system would be the use of four-count phrases inserted among the sets of eight. An example of this is the "Crapshooters' Dance" from *Guys and Dolls.* The dance music and the variations are based on the melody of the song "Luck Be a Lady." Since it is derived from a song, the variation is built on the thirty-two-count block system. However, between the major blocks, four counts (two measures of music) are added to aid the transition from block to block and from key to key. These, of course, must be accounted for in terms of the counts used by the dancers. Looking at the opening portion of the "Crapshooters' Dance," we now find:

Counts:	16	(2 × 8)	Introduction
	32	(4 × 8)	Theme A
	4		*transition*
	32	(4 × 8)	Theme A
	4		*transition*

32	(4 × 8)	Theme B
32	(4 × 8)	Theme A
4		*transition*
32	(4 × 8)	Theme B
32	(4 × 8)	Theme A

If a musical phrase does not take a full eight counts, as with the four-count passages in the "Crapshooters' Dance," the counting ends when the new phrase begins: "1-2-3-4-5-6-7-8, 1-2-3-4, 1-2-3-4-5-6-7-8," and so on. As the excerpt from the "Crapshooters' Dance" below illustrates, the count system is based on what is required by the sound of the music.

"Crapshooters' Dance" excerpt from *Guys and Dolls* *

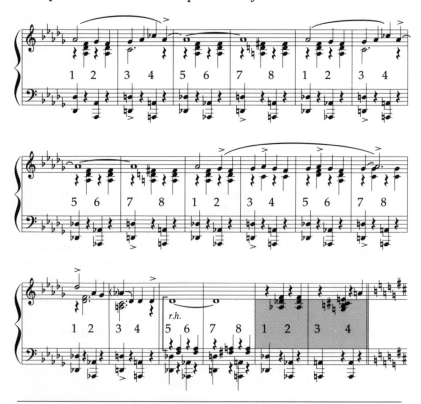

Phrases Without Patterns

Though almost all music is counted at a steady beat, the musical phrases do not have to fit into an eight- or four-count mold, nor into any consistent pattern at all. Looking at the "Soldier-Sailor" segment from *On the Town*'s "Miss Turnstiles Ballet," we find the soldier's theme established, followed by the sailor's, in this sequence of phrases:

Counts:	4		Introductory Vamp
	24	(8 + 6 + 10)	Soldier's Theme
	24	(3 × 8)	Sailor's Theme
	8		Soldier's Theme
	6		Sailor's Theme
	6		Soldier's Theme
	6		Sailor's Theme
	20	(2 × 8 + 4)	Variations

Although the soldier's theme is introduced in twenty-four counts, its phrasing does not divide evenly into three convenient sets of eight, but is structured as an eight, a six, and a ten, melodically. The choreographer must acknowledge this count system if the choreography is going to relate to the sound of the music.

The next twenty-four counts establish the sailor's theme, the count system being in three even eights. After the sailor's theme, the two themes alternate as an eight followed by three sets of six, causing each one, when heard, to give the impression that it is interrupting its predecessor. In interpreting the music, we can sense from this back-and-forth motion of the melodies that either Miss Turnstiles is going from one man to the other, or that the men alternately are coming to her.

What happens if the *time signature* changes during the course of the piece? Here, the beat continues as steadily as ever, unless a change is indicated, but the new number of beats in the measures may alter the length or shape of the phrases. These occasions should always be highlighted somehow in the score to remind the choreographer of the shift.

Rhythmic Alteration

Sometimes, a definite feeling of rhythmic alteration will emerge as the choreographer follows the score. A new timing factor is making its presence known, in which case one continues to count, marking the passage in the score accordingly, knowing that *this* is the place where such change occurs. The excerpt from *Carousel*'s "Ballet" on page 47 illustrates how a new timing can appear in the music. In other instances, the rhythmic alteration may be so subtle that the time change is relayed only to the musician performing the piece, leaving the average listener unaware of such a construction.

Tempo and the Choreographic Beat

Lastly, the choreographer must concern himself with dance tempos which do not correspond to the rhythm or speed as defined by the time signature.

The composer has his own reasons for employing a given signature: to enable future musicians to correctly reproduce the intricacies of the composition. The given tempo, however, may not correspond with a beat that is suitable for choreography. A 4/4 time signature played quickly can feel more like a slow 2/4, as "Many a New Day" from *Oklahoma!* illustrates. This perky tune has flippant triplets that perfectly represent Laurey's denial of pain; the essence of the song lies in her false gaiety, smoothly delivered, yet insistent. The music must proceed at a brisk clip to convey such a mood and at a time value of C (4/4). "Many a New Day"'s note values count out as shown on page 48.

As an experiment, count aloud at the rate of speed that the song suggests and try some movements around the room while maintaining that tempo. The rapid 1-2-3-4 pattern will prove too fast for a comfortable walking pace. Also, most jumps, turns, and dance movements will gravitate toward the first and third beats—1-2-3-4—or the second and fourth beats, thus taking *two* such beats to execute. In computing the dance speed, the choreographer would find "Many a New Day"'s tempo more serviceable by halving the quick four beats per measure, as illustrated on page 49.

"Ballet" excerpt from *Carousel* *

(Announces upcoming change)

"Many a New Day" excerpt from *Oklahoma!* *

Phrases in 3/4 Time

There is a common exception to the above examples: the counting of phrases in 3/4 time. Musical statements in this time signature usually occur over the length of eight *measures,* as opposed to eight *beats.* With three beats to a bar, one would guess that it takes twenty-four beats to complete an ordinary phrase, but this is not the way to count these statements. In most cases, the accent, or strongest feeling of the sound, falls on the first beat of each measure, and it is on that beat that the count system is based. Allowing three beats per measure, as in 1-2-3, 1-2-3, we see on page 50 that the sequence in the "Dream Ballet" from *Oklahoma!* is held by keeping track of the first beat of each measure, until the phrase ends ($\underline{1}$-2-3, $\underline{2}$-2-3, $\underline{3}$-2-3, $\underline{4}$-2-3, and so on).

The Count System: Summary

In these first explorations of the score, the numbers for counts which the choreographer sets down in his copy are not necessarily the beats per measure as indicated in the time signature. What the choreographer is listening for are the number of foot-counts required by each individual phrase as paced at a comfortable rate of speed. These counts usually do fall on the musical beat, or divisions thereof, and the numbers should be marked in the appropriate measures of the score. The count system must also take into account any variations in timing: in addition to his notation system, the choreographer should add the word or symbol for "and" (=) between counts to signify double time and "and-a" (+ a) to signify triple time. Later, individual steps and equivalents, such as timed leaps, will be matched and notated to the established count system. The counts the choreographer uses to teach the routine in rehearsal are these same phrasing counts found in his score.

"Dream Ballet" excerpt from *Oklahoma!* *

MELODY LINE AND VARIATIONS

As soon as possible, the choreographer should trace the notes that signify the *melody* line. Whatever is occurring in the musical arrangement, the choreographer will create his movements along a predominantly-heard "through-line." If the choreographer can follow the course of the melody and count out the timings of the phrases, the score is within his grasp for his needs.

The melody can only move up, down, or at a constant pitch. It is a simple matter to follow along, even if one is unfamiliar with the sounds of the different intervals between the notes.

When looking at the printed page of music, the melody will usually be the top note in the structure, most often to be found in the treble clef, but occasionally in the bass clef. Below, we see a version of the song "If I Loved You" as it appears in the opening of *Carousel*'s second-act ballet. The melody is shown as the top line of notes supported by clear chords, and the time between the melody notes is filled with rolling arpeggios.

In the excerpt from *The King and I*'s "Getting to Know You" on page 52, the melody is repeated in the bass clef.

In both of these illustrations, previous familiarity with the songs helps in identifying and locating the right notes on the staff. It is also helpful to have the lyrics coupled with the music.

The example on page 53 shows another instance of the melody in the bass clef, as found in the song "Shipoopi" from *The Music Man*.

"If I Loved You" excerpt from *Carousel* *

"Getting to Know You" excerpt from *The King and I* *

"Shipoopi" excerpt from *The Music Man* *

This melody has not been heard in the show before, serving only as a minor variation to the dance steps. At first glance, the theme could move either upward or downward in pitch. Both clefs begin with a feel of accompaniment, then the functions of the treble and bass clefs are reversed. When the treble clef is read through, the choreographer will see that it merely contains pairs of triads per measure on every other beat, holding the rhythm and key. The more diverse activity is happening in the bass line.

Variations can actually take two forms: (1) different musical treatments of the original melody, or (2) music not heard before at all.

The former type of variation may stem from changing the rhythm, key, dynamics, or orchestration. A variation consisting of music not previously heard, however, will introduce a new melody and theme. In the end, the choreographer must remember that every bit of music in a score will have a recognizable melody.

BLOCKS

After the choreographer has marked the counts according to phrases and melody lines, he must then mark off groups of phrases into blocks denoting larger sections of the choreography. Each of these blocks represents a self-contained idea in which a single theme, mood, or variation finds expression, yet is also only one part of the entire dance number. These blocks, which often reflect the "A-A-B-A" patterns that are used in songs, can be made of *any* length of music in the show and grouped into sections to express larger thoughts.

The division of blocks should flow naturally from the sound of the music and the progression of the dramatic stages of the piece, signalling general changes in the dance. A good example of this sense of change is the excerpt from the "Farmer Dance" on page 61, in which the individual blocks consist of sets of eight counts. Each set has its own distinctive sound, and is treated as a separate entity within the whole.

In the notation process, the choreographer needs to outline the beginning, ending, and general content of each block.

MOMENTS AND SHIFTS

The choreographer must also note in the score any special moments in the music or any shift of mood or theme. A *moment* will often signal some dramatic event, and commands the audience's attention at the time it occurs. A moment may interrupt the regular flow of the melody line, be placed between completed themes, or serve as part of the musical climax.

A moment may be highlighted in the score. For example, the climactic chords in *West Side Story*'s rumble scene correspond exactly with a dramatic action—Bernardo piercing A-rab's ear, Bernardo killing Riff, and Tony killing Bernardo in a moment of impassioned revenge. These events are actually spelled out where the chords occur in the score. Sometimes, moments are not given any written significance at all, leaving all interpretation up to the ingenuity of the choreographer.

The score can also indicate an abrupt transition, an unprepared breaking from one mood to another, to signify that some dramatic event has occurred. A sudden, drastic *shift* will take the audience by surprise, giving them a jolt of uncertainty instead of a comfortable acclimation. Mood shifts should be marked in the score to remind the choreographer that there is such a change, and to identify the dynamics of the sounds involved.

CHOREOGRAPHIC CLUES

On occasion, specific or general inconsistencies in the score can serve as choreographic guideposts. Even if no choreographic or dramatic footnote is supplied in the score, the mere sound of these inconsistencies will hint at structurally choreographic elements. Consider how the intermittent rests and pauses in *Carousel's* "Hornpipe" music can be used choreographically, as illustrated on page 56.

In this example, we have two different kinds of clues: a wood block struck on the beat (shown by the x's) and silences which obviously interrupt the melodic progression. Although these silences are not consistent, they are not arbitrarily placed. The contemporary choreographer cannot ignore their presence, for neither will the audience. The question now for the choreographer is: how are the silences to be used?

Another example of inconsistent sounds that offer choreographic clues would be the measure of wood-block sounds simulating the shaking of dice in the "Crapshooters' Dance" from *Guys and Dolls* (page 57).

Here, the composer has provided an explanation: "Shaking dice—Wood Block (Dice effect)." The choreographer has several options. He can stage the dance so that the wood-block sounds correspond with the men shaking dice—in this case, the choreographer must have the dancers in the right positions at the right moment. Yet the choreographer may want to use the wood-block sounds for some other movement, or leave out this sound effect altogether.

CHANGING THE MUSIC

So far in this chapter, the discussion has centered on working with the score "as is." However, "as is" really means that the music was shaped to suit dance movements in the original production. Though the choreographer must work with the

"Hornpipe" excerpt from *Carousel* *

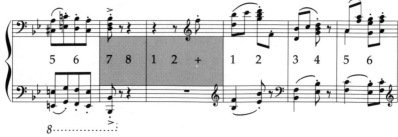

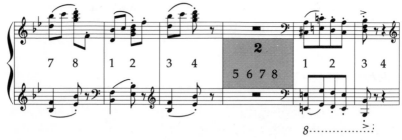

"Crapshooters' Dance" excerpt from *Guys and Dolls* *

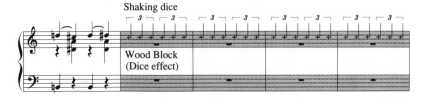

music as written, there are still fresh uses available for the shadings, accents, and speeds indicated in the score.

The scoring was dictated by the original choreography, the size of that first company's stage, the abilities of the original performers, and any number of other technical considerations. Since none of those conditions will be duplicated for the production at hand, alterations will be necessary to bring the essence of the original production to the new situation.

The choreographer must ask himself: what functions does the number fulfill structurally and dramatically in the production? If the number is supposed to cover for a change of set or scenery, it must be long enough to provide the time necessary for the change—and, in an amateur situation, even more time might be needed. If the number serves to help pacing, it may have to be reduced to come within the grasp of the amateur ensemble's abilities.

There are really only two ways to adapt the printed score to fit present circumstances (not counting adding/ transplanting accents, or transposing the pitch of a number). These adjustments are shortening and lengthening.

Shortening the Music

In many cases, the choreographer may wish to cut back on the amount of the material to be tackled. Why? Because a shorter, cleaner, fast-moving, well-varied number is always preferable to a sloppily-executed and repetitive time-filler. Whatever the reason for shortening, the advantage is the same: the less to be created and learned, the better it can be perfected. The performers' time can be spent in refining the smaller quantity toward higher quality.

Shortening music is a necessary evil, because novices require much more time to master the dance material than is available. Even professional companies now have so little time to learn their workload that the choice must be made between precise execution *versus* full-length execution. Professional performers learn their full quota *and* refine their movements only in large Broadway-size revivals and on tours.

Today's choreographer is under no obligation to use all of the music. The original production may have called for more music than the current situation can effectively utilize, and the current production may not need all of the original phrases, blocks, and themes to make its desired statement. Music should not be filled with movement simply because the music is there. Indeed, the music should be cut by the choreographer if he cannot use it, and if it is not essential to the overall plot. If no orchestra is being used in the performances, the piano reduction may seem uncomfortably repetitive during some of the dance music—another justification for eliminating unwanted sections.

To shorten a number as a whole, cuts are made internally within the structure of the piece; these cuts can range from single measures to whole thematic blocks. One important rule always prevails: any and all alterations must sound musically correct to the ear. That is to say, changes must never draw attention to themselves.

I once witnessed a horrendous example of shortening at a college production of *Guys and Dolls*. In one of the numbers, three young men did steps back and forth for a while. Then, the dancers and the music suddenly stopped—the band had finished playing at the point where the choreographer had run out of steps! The choreographer had made no attempt to effectively cut and piece together different sections in order to create an abbreviated yet complete-sounding number.

For an example of the proper way to shorten a number, let's look at the "Crapshooters' Dance" from *Guys and Dolls*. The choreographer might face a problem of having to structure a dance under conditions where male dancers, much less a full stage of them, are at an absolute premium. Here is the key to the solution: while a musical theme must be established for the variations to have any meaning or make sense, the theme does not have to be repeated over and over once it has been established. The music can be trimmed and sections of the piece divided among the men so that they *all* do not have to learn steps choreographed to *all* of the music.

The "Crapshooters' Dance"'s musical themes are taken from the different parts of the song "Luck Be a Lady." Altogether, the number runs to 259 measures. The opening eight bars serve as introductory (curtain-opening) music. The next seventy bars offer the "A-A-B-A" refrain of the song, including pairs of transitional measures between thematic blocks. At measure 79, however, the final blocks "B" and "A" (starting from the latter half of "B") are repeated again, exactly as they had been before. The earliest dispensable material would be these repeats, along with the transitional bars which introduced them. Thus, the choreographer could cut from measure 77 through measure 110—a reduction of 34 bars!

The dance music itself runs from measure 111 to measure 150. This music, previously unplayed in the score, is exclusively for choreographic use, and is unrelated to the song itself. Again, in this music, the final four bars repeat. The second set is constructed to make the transition into the next section. The first set can be eliminated with no apparent harm. The *verse* of the song now makes its initial appearance melodically from measures 151 to 178, adding a new sound, but, once again, the "B" and "A" blocks of the refrain are repeated. The choreographer can remove these blocks, too. Cuts have then been made from measures 179 to 210. The rest of the number provides building variations on the basic "A" theme, "Luck Be a Lady," until the climax and ending of the piece.

In making these three simple cuts of repeated material, the choreographer has shortened the music by some 72 measures, approximately a quarter of its length. He can examine the structure of the music even more closely and make further, more intricate streamlining cuts. The true test of any cut is its invisibility. Does the music sound as though nothing is missing or contrived? One of the best ways to answer the question is to have someone who has not been involved in the cutting process listen to the music and offer an honest opinion.

The easiest, quickest, and most obvious changes in music can be made by eliminating, transplanting, or shortening structural blocks. Many times, a section of music will be written to be played and then repeated with what is called a "second ending," which either resolves the melody or makes the necessary transition to the next part. The excerpt from *Oklahoma!*'s "Farmer Dance" on page 61 illustrates this second ending.

The choreographer may choose to eliminate the first ending and move directly to the second. However, there may be times when he will want to use both endings to create a certain mood.

Once the choreographer has recommended what should be cut, it is the music director's job to know how to engineer these changes. A word of caution: overzealous cutting can make the music sound a trifle skimpy.

Lengthening

Since the production at hand will have different technical requirements than those of the original stage production, the choreographer may have to lengthen a particular piece of music. For example, the stage area may be too large to accomplish the steps within a given framework, as with the ballet from *The King and I*, where the stage must be crossed again and again within set phrases of music. There may be the need to cover for complete scene changes, or to resolve dramatic

"Farmer Dance" excerpt from *Oklahoma!* *

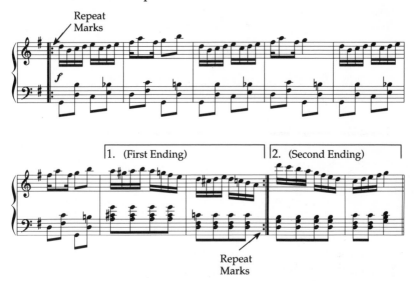

action with full effect, when the original amount of music will not do so. The choreographer may also want to expand the opportunity to exhibit the performers' talents—though fledgling choreographers often have enough trouble creating imaginative sequences around the music they already have without adding more movements to their load.

The best way to lengthen a piece is to extend what is already supplied, rather than write and arrange original compositions to augment the score. If an extension is minor, individual phrases, or parts thereof, may be repeated, or an introductory/background vamp can be inserted. As with the process of shortening the music, *any* additions or alterations must sound musically correct and not call attention to themselves; they should never just sound stuck in or be needlessly redundant. If the number requires much more time than allotted, the choreographer can restructure the piece by transplanting whole blocks. Instead of repeating identical blocks back-to-back, stagger the blocks or vary the melody, accent, rhythm, or accompaniment of certain blocks. *Never use the same music more than two times in a row.*

---

5 MUSICAL STAGING

L ooking at the possibilities that both the script and the score offer the choreographer leads us to the topic of musical staging. Musical staging involves not only creating dance numbers, but also arranging those gestures and movements performed during the delivery of a song. This latter type of musical staging can consume a great deal of the choreographer's time: because a musical comedy score contains far more material for singing than for dancing, "choreography" in this case is not limited to just dancing. Even if a soloist does nothing but stand or sit in one place for the duration of the piece, this event must be classified as staging because it was both decided upon and directed that way. Distinctions between staging and pure dance can be murky: choreographic dance footwork frequently appears in staging, while dramatic, literal, and lyrical gestures are often used in purely dance segments. In general, dance alone has far fewer qualifying factors to consider than movement created to supplement vocal work.

Musical staging represents the broadest range of presentational possibilities, from the quietest moment of solitary introspection to a stage full of people loudly belting a song. Here the choreographer must assume the secondary role of stage director, framing intimate and dramatic moments in the context of a song's music and lyrics. When creating dance movements alone, the choreographer draws solely from the music and the dramatic situation; in musical staging, however, the *words* being sung receive priority.

Just as the musical numbers aid the progression of the show, staging provides a flow to the musical numbers. One cautionary note must always be remembered: make sure a song is not "overstaged." The song's vocal and aural impact may be powerful enough to render representative dance movement superfluous. Additionally, the choreographer must take care to apply the same style that is being used for the rest of the production.

Songs come in all shapes and sizes, written to fill any variety of functions, and to be performed by any range of persons, from solos to full ensembles. Yet every song in a musical comedy score is there for a reason, and to create dance designations for these songs, the choreographer must look at each one and ask himself: Does the song introduce, declare, clarify, describe, offer commentary, or consist of on-the-spot action? Is it intended to be humorous, serious, or narrative? Is anything supposed to occur over the course of the song which is important to the plot or which will be referred to later?

SONG STRUCTURE

Because each song serves a particular function in the context of the show, the choreographer must, at the outset, know how the song is constructed and how its music and lyrics work together. Musical numbers must be smoothly integrated with their surrounding material, so in the vast majority of cases, the transition from spoken dialogue to song and dance is accomplished through introductory music and a vocal introduction.

The introductory music is often a subtle underscoring beneath the dialogue, which is leading toward the premise of the piece. The sung introduction (the verse) follows, putting forth what the song proper (refrain) will be about. The diagram on page 64 illustrates how the song relates to the dramatic material surrounding it.

Every song will have a beginning, a middle, and an end. While the song's beginning must be graceful enough so that

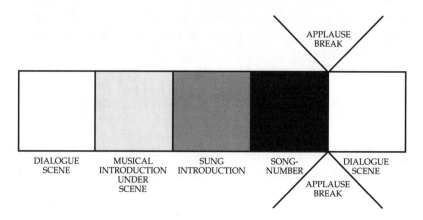

APPLAUSE
BREAK

DIALOGUE | MUSICAL | SUNG | SONG- | DIALOGUE
SCENE | INTRODUCTION | INTRODUCTION | NUMBER | SCENE
UNDER		
SCENE		APPLAUSE
		BREAK

"here comes a song!" is not abruptly trumpeted, the ending should be rousing enough to add to a sense of emotional excitement and resolution. Most songs are written to gradually build to a climax before restoration of dramatic action.

To provide this effect, both the melodic line of the songs and the context of the dances is altered near the end to heighten the impact. Musically, this finale is accomplished by pitch escalation or by delaying the musical resolution, causing a higher tension and, thus, a greater relief when it arrives. The piece may be lengthened at the last stretch before the ending and constructed in either a repetitive pattern or an ascending pattern, for added excitement.

For a repetitive pattern, the additional music must be filled with lyrics in order to restate the message of the piece in more emphatic terms. The most elementary form is the basic repeat, which reinforces what has been said. This device is used to end four popular songs from *Guys and Dolls*:

> That the guy's only doing it
> For some doll
> Some doll
> Some doll
> The guy's only doing it for
> Some doll!
>
> Luck be a lady
>   (Luck be a lady—instrumental)

Luck be a lady
  (Luck be a lady—instrumental)
Luck–be–a–la–dy,
To–ni–i–i–i–i–ght

Sit down, you're rockin'
Sit down, sit down,
Sit down, you're rockin' the boat.
Sit down, you're rockin'
Sit down, sit down
Sit down, you're rockin' the boat.
Sit down—you're rockin'—the boat!

Marry the man today,
And change his ways,
And change his ways,
And change his ways,
And change his ways,
And change his ways,
Tomorrow!

The device of repetitive patterns is also used in five songs in *My Fair Lady*: "Why Can't the English," "With a Little Bit of Luck," "Get Me to the Church on Time," "Wouldn't It Be Loverly?", and "I Could Have Danced All Night."

When used to complete a piece, *pitch escalation* occurs at a constant rate within a brief period of time. To match the escalation, the lyrics tend to become more list-like in nature, presenting a series of adjectives or ideas expanding the theme. At the end of "Mr. Snow," Carrie summarizes its subject with: "That *young*, seafarin', *bold* and darin', *big*, bewhiskered, *overbearin'*—darlin' Mr. Snow," perfectly reflecting the upward course of the melody.

A more complex example is the closing line of "Iowa Stubborn" from *The Music Man*, shown on page 66.

The title song of *Oklahoma!* (page 66) goes so far as to spell out what it is all about.

The ending of a number is a most important concern. The audience, hopefully, applauds after virtually every song or dance segment, totally interrupting the proceedings. The ending should not only tell the audience when to applaud (this

"Iowa Stubborn" excerpt from *The Music Man* *

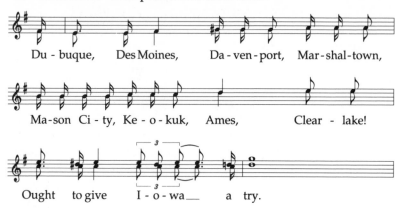

may seem obvious, but have you ever been in the awkward situation of not being sure if a number is finished or not?), but also stir the viewers to *want* to applaud (hence the additional dynamics). The ending functions as the last point of the particular illusion before dramatic action resumes, and creates the final, lasting impression that the audience takes home with them.

In terms of movement, the throwing-out of fully extended arms, lifting of girls into abruptly frozen poses, or sudden striking of an ensemble tableau are all commonly accepted cues for an ending. In all cases, the final action must recap, top, and finalize all that has gone before it. And, most importantly, any action must end *precisely* with the music.

Of course, there are exceptions where a few songs and dances do not end in the conventional show-stopping way:

"Oklahoma" excerpt from *Oklahoma!***

---

* Lyrics by Oscar Hammerstein II, Music by Richard Rodgers. Copyright © 1943 by Williamson Music Co. Copyright Renewed. International Copyright Secured. All Rights Reserved.

** Music and Lyrics by Meredith Willson. © 1950, 1954, 1958 Frank Music Corp. and Meredith Willson Music. © Renewed 1978, 1982, 1986 Frank Music Corp. and Meredith Willson Music. International Copyright Secured. All Rights Reserved. Used by Permission.

West Side Story's "I Have a Love" and *Brigadoon*'s "Funeral Dance," to name two. Serious in intention and context, they are structured to discourage applause by fading out or immediately returning to the plot.

LYRIC VS. MUSIC

The lyric and the music each has its own message. Lyrics concern the literal and the emotional, while the music evokes feelings, all of which are influenced by tempo, rhythm, accent, and dynamics. While the lyric consists of *what* a character is saying, the music tells us *how* he is saying it. The music qualifies the statement of the words, while at the same time acting to convey their meaning. Music can support and extend the mood of the lyric, or contradict it to create a multiple or confused sentiment.

One way to test the relationship of words to music is for the choreographer to approach a given song as totally separated from the music. What do the words alone say? If put to another piece of music with the same time signature, does their meaning prevail or does the mood change? By the same token, if the music is presented without a vocal—just with melody and arrangement—what impressions does it convey?

In the majority of cases, the lyric and music support each other. And in terms of subject matter, most scores tend to focus on love's exuberance and its opposites.

Conditions become a little more interesting, however, when the sound contradicts the verbal sentiment either by directly or by subtly undercutting the truth of the words. The song "People Will Say We're in Love," for example, seems to be a flat denial of affection, with lyrics like "Don't throw bouquets at me" and "Don't please my folks too much." But the flowing, harmonic structure of the music tells the listener that there is, indeed, love between these two people. We can hear that they do not mean what they say, in and through the music. Imagine the different effect the song would have if the melody had a driving beat or otherwise expressed angry adamancy.

Another type of treatment is using the music to enliven a depressing situation. In *Show Boat*'s "Life on the Wicked

Stage," the woes and sad truths of a theatrical existence are lightened into a knowing savvy by a bright, coquettish tune. The simultaneous use of opposing dynamics can produce intentionally comedic results, as in "Shy" from *Once Upon a Mattress,* where the lyrics say "meek and mild," but the melody blares "raucous surprise!"

A blend of lyrical statement and melodic mood can produce a multilevel message, providing a nice degree of subtlety. "I'll Be Wearing Ribbons Down My Back" from *Hello, Dolly!* is a good example, for while Irene Malloy's words are hopeful, the mode of their expression is wistful.

A song may also contradict its surrounding dramatic circumstances by expressing an emotion quite different from the mood of the character performing the song—as when *The King and I's* Anna, to disguise her fear, sings "I Whistle a Happy Tune," or when *Oklahoma!'s* Laurey hides her anger and hurt with "Many a New Day." These contradictory songs pose more interesting possibilities in staging because of the different levels of statement being conveyed. The challenge lies in providing glimpses of the emotion which the material seeks to conceal or control. For example, Anna and Louis *do* cheer up from "I Whistle a Happy Tune," and Laurey's facade is a bit less wholehearted in "Many a New Day."

Of course, here, too, there may be shades of gray. In *Camelot's* "What Do the Simple Folk Do?", the focus swings back and forth between boredom and its cures. *The Pajama Game's* "I'm Not at All in Love" offers a lilting waltz with defiant words. The wry humor emerges from Babe's not knowing that she does not believe her words, though everyone else recognizes her condition but her.

The choreographer has to be alert to the inner meanings of a song; some lyrics express mild sarcasm beneath a charming and sentimental surface, generating a humorous response from the audience. For example, delicate femininity is equated with domestic drudgery in *Hello, Dolly!'s* "It Takes a Woman." In a similar vein, *Camelot's* "Simple Joys of Maidenhood" is a light, frothy prayer, a song sent up by a princess-figure hoping for the medieval "normalities" of blood, death, and carnage.

Further examination of the elements of a song brings us to the "triple-split": lyrics do one thing, the melody another, and the musical arrangement and the accompaniment suggest a third idea. *Bells Are Ringing*'s "Just in Time" presents such a construction. The lyrics are romantic, declaring that the lovers have found each other "just in time." The major part of the melody is very straight, redundant, and relatively expressionless. Two notes are played back and forth in succession until the second-to-last note in the phrase introduces a third pitch. The song gets its jaunty style, making it both interesting and dramatically appropriate, from the musical treatment *under* its theme.

Looking at *Bells Are Ringing*, we see how "Just in Time" fits into a larger picture. The major plot concerns Ella Peterson (high energy, optimistic, naive) and Jeff Moss (externally cocky, internally insecure). Her songs are all perky and forthright; his songs tend toward the jazzier, playboy style. These qualities for both characters are maintained throughout the first act, until the two finally share an undisguisedly tender romantic ballad which closes the curtain.

When we next see Ella and Jeff together in the second act, their relationship must be re-established after the intermission—and now that their "serious love" has been declared, it is time to lighten the situation with some comfortable fun. The result is "Just in Time," serious in intent, but kept casual through Jeff's jazzy delivery and buoyant by Ella's injection of humor.

Structurally, the song is sandwiched between two chorus numbers. While giving the audience a change from the larger ensemble staging, the tone of the number does not allow the pacing to drop. "Just in Time" reaches a wonderful range of levels through variations in song and dance following the initial statement: solo, duet, chorus, harmony, stop time, patter, and humor. The sequence consistently conveys an honest message through playful antics, from its sincere beginning through its stroll-into-the-sunset-with-Hollywood-chorus romantic ending. Most numbers in musical comedies are similarly multi-purposed.

CHOREOGRAPHY IN MUSICAL STAGING

Not all songs require lengthy analysis; most songs are obvious in their purpose and meaning, and once these are grasped, staging can take place. Sometimes, just as stage directions and choreographic notes may be provided in the script, various degrees of staging notes may be parenthetically included in the music to the song. These notes are meant to indicate movements which were originally matched to a given word or phrase. They may be followed, ignored, or simply used as guides.

When devising the choreographic movements for the people on stage, there are seven areas, physically and visually, that need to be monitored.

Body placement and travel concerns both the static use and movement of the human figure. The choreographer needs to determine where the figure is on stage at different moments in the song, how he relates spatially to other performers and set pieces, and when these spatial relationships change. The choreographer must also ask: What is the figure doing with his body at various points in the delivery—is he standing, sitting, kneeling, lying, or leaning? When does his body change position? At what angle should the actor's body face the audience and other performers during various sections of the material? When the performer moves from one place to another, how far the actor travels (a single step or a full-stage cross), and where he goes, are equally important considerations.

Focus refers to the aim and the target of delivery. Who is the number being sung to—a specific individual, onstage crowd, or the audience? Attention must be paid to audibility and visibility. Performers should not be directed to sing to each other in absolute profile or turn upstage with their backs to the audience. Without always facing each other, actors have to create the illusion of onstage communication, while remaining open for audience access.

Gestures need to be clearly perceived from great distances. The placement of hands, fingers, and thumbs must be clean and distinct. Delivery should be executed precisely without movements appearing stiff. With those movements extending outward from the body, the energy must seem to radiate down to and through the hands and fingertips. It is the energized, committed figure and gesture which will inspire response from the viewers. Limp movements will read as if the character himself is weak or that he does not feel strongly about the subject matter.

Another area of concern is *props*. What furniture or other large objects are to be required by the script? Can all the props be used? Besides the hand props included through stage direction or dramatic necessity, the choreographer should be able to introduce additional items which naturally lend themselves to the situation.

Choreography during a song can range from an occasionally designed step to full dance breaks. Many numbers are constructed like this: the song is sung through once, and then repeated. In the second rendition, however, the first half of the song or so is played as an instrumental to be filled with stage business or choreography, until the vocal with choreography is resumed for the wrap-up of the number.

Two factors help differentiate between musical staging and choreography: the complexity of the dance movement and the vocabulary from which it is drawn. If a character is to execute a "grapevine" (a series of alternating cross steps), quick spin, or a tap step during his vocal delivery, we see these as choreographic in quality. What can blur the distinction between "staging" and "choreography" is the extent and context of the movement. The "Big Spender" girls in *Sweet Charity* certainly use their full bodies and limbs while singing. Would one call this "choreography," "musical staging," "staged choreography," or "choreographic staging"? In this instance, the differences may only be nominal.

There is no ironclad rule pertaining to the use or distribution of gestures and movements during a song. Some dance schools teach, "If you say it, don't do it." While this approach may spare audiences dance translations of the lyric, it does not allow for the perfectly illustrative gestures which accompany ordinary speech. What could be more natural then for Curly to sit himself down next to Laurey while spinning the fantasy of the "Surrey with the Fringe on Top"?

The choreographer must also regulate the *pacing* of movements. While variety and surprise are always desirable for sustaining interest, both motivation and circumstances will dictate the level of acceptability. The commonplace advice "moderation in all things" would seem to be a safe guide. Too many actions can become distracting and weaken the general presentation. A few well-placed, clearly defined ventures in travel and positioning, augmented by gestures at key moments, will add the support sought for the sentiment.

What *framework of movement* is being employed in the production—do the performers move in a natural or stylized manner? As with stage acting, natural movements and reactions imitated stylistically may not carry the desired message to the audience. But actions and gestures executed in too small a fashion can become lost or may be difficult to perceive clearly. Therefore, some exaggeration of the material must be taken into consideration.

At the other end of the spectrum, the choreographer may have to deal with the completely stylized treatment, which does not pretend to represent ordinary life at all. Whether done as satire or fantasy, these movements must still be identifiable. Though recognizable in everyday existence as unusual, the stylized gestures and staging elements can work effectively as long as they make sense within the "world of the show." The movements must transmit the same message through stylization as would be conveyed in life by natural means. No matter how far from "ordinary life" a situation is depicted, it must remain easily decipherable by the audience.

Between slightly exaggerated naturalism (basic theatrical staging) and extreme stylization, the choreographer will have to deal with many gradations in between, from subtle nuance to blatantly slapstick routines. How does one know how far to go in staging? The answer will vary from artist to artist; it is this sense of "how much is too much" which separates one choreographer from another. Ultimately, the audience will judge the craft of the choreographer by their acceptance or rejection of the total production.

In devising staging for an ensemble, the choreographer must take into account the variety of *physical types* assembled; the challenge is to minimize or blend the spectrum of bodies, for a short, chunky body simply will not move in the same way as a long, lean torso. Similarly, creating staging for an individual means viewing the performer as actually two entities—a character making a statement, and an actor delivering the piece. While all the gestures, steps, and travel patterns must reflect and extend a character as known by the audience, the staging must also be constructed not only to make the number work, but also to make the performer look good. No matter how wonderful a vision of the production the choreographer may have in his mind's eye, he must adapt to the physical strengths and weaknesses of the person who will execute the material, and meet the creative challenge of matching the right performers to the right body movements.

6 STRUCTURING A DANCE NUMBER

Just as every dance number has a dramatic and structural purpose in the overall scheme of the show, every movement *within* the number should have both a dramatic and structural *raison d'etre*. Whether the choreographer is working with or against the music—which, with its progression of themes, moods, and events, dictates when incidents occur and how long they transpire—it is the musical sequence's dramatic premise which is the foundation of the dance movements.

Each dance number resembles a short one-act play in several respects. In both the dance number and the one-act play, the audience begins in ignorance of what is to come. Ideas must be cogently presented, strongly developed, and convincingly resolved over the duration of the piece. The format follows the formula of the well-made play: exposition, rising action, climax, and fall to ending. The brief time element of a musical number, however, usually does not allow much time for dénouement.

Every musical comedy must have a plot to maintain audience interest, as well as another crucial element—a sense of conflict. Within the dance number itself, the musical variations that create this sense of conflict maintain the audience's interest because they interfere with and delay a resolution. The choreographer must explore the dramatic and structural factors which prevent the character or plot from moving to point A, and then on to point B. A simple crossing of the stage can become an entire drama if the path is continually blocked and the hero hindered by various means. Choreographically speaking, *why* does anything happen in spite of hindrances? The reasons and motivations of the characters must be apparent for the piece to make any sense or elicit an empathic response.

The element of surprise, which can both delight and terrify, is also important for holding the audience's attention. But just as the music is limited by its own rules of content and progress, so, too, are dance elements restricted by the "givens" or "expectations" of the production and the style of the presentation. Dramatic validity sets the boundaries: no matter how great a "bit" or step seems, if it is wrong for the time, place, character, or situation, it should not be used.

When we speak of structuring a dance number, we are really talking about organizing and presenting several visual, emotional, and dramatic elements. These elements fall into five major categories—music; grouping; floor planning; rising energy and climaxes; and beginnings and endings.

MUSIC

The choreographer examines the music closely for any type of "plot line" which relates to the general story of the show. Is the piece there only to create a certain mood or illustrate a song? If the music seems to offer no "plot line," can one be created out of the onstage characters, setting, and situation?

The music should be constantly listened to, and re-listened to, for different purposes throughout the development of the choreography. Initially, the music should be heard as a work unto itself, divorced from the printed score and the choreographer's dance-step markings (which will be used later). Questions like the following will start to arise: Considering the situation from which the music arises in the script, what feelings does the sound of the music evoke? What does it seem to describe? Does it suggest a secondary story line which has not been previously supplied? Does the music suggest the presence of a specific character, or a mood/melody/motif that is recognizable as his? What dynamics are at work? Do some sections sound busier, more massive, or more simplistic than others?

Once the musical variations have been identified, any of the choreographer's impressions and findings should be marked and labeled in the score *after* the counts, phrases, and blocks have been indicated. At this point, the choreographer begins noting how the dance movements will work with the music. If the dance works *against* the music, the results can be dramatic. For example, the choreographer can work the dance steps against the mood of the music to show inner turmoil, conflict, confusion, or effort. If the dance steps work against the tempo (slow steps to fast music, or vice versa), the results can be equally effective for the viewers. Excitement and intricacy can also be added to the choreography by working rhythms against each other. For example, the choreographer could match movement patterns that take four counts to music that is written in three-count time.

One must be very careful in matching steps to the music. While it is being played, the music exerts a subtle yet pervasive influence, and ultimately seems the stronger power in comparison to the visual scenes. For example, a figure doing quick steps to slow, ponderous music will seem to be fighting some great burden. If the dancer slows down and the music does not change, the music will seem to have won the conflict.

How literally should the choreographer interpret the score? Moderation is the key here. Too close an alignment with the music, where every musical turn is perfectly mirrored by gesture, can become boring, but obviously, too little coordination between movement and the music will seem confusing.

The guideposts for structuring movement are (1) those notes in the script which specify certain movements, and (2) those moments marked in the score which call for dramatic actions. If the choreographer is adding his own scenarios to those parts of the music which will need to have content supplied, the key moments in the music that signify those plotted incidents should be well-marked.

GROUPING

Creating grouping patterns and a floor plan (which will show where groups of performers are and where they are to move) can be done at roughly the same time. A "group" is defined as any fraction of the total active ensemble—both a soloist and the rest of the ensemble can be a group. More precisely, a group is any division of the performers who are used alternatingly in a musical number, either in terms of time (Group B dances when Group A is finished) or space (Group A dances over to stage right while Group B dances over to stage left).

The term "group," then, refers to a set of one or more performers at a particular spot on the stage, and "grouping" to the technique by which sets of dancers perform different sections of a musical number at different times. In contrast to grouping, *total unison work* calls for all the performers to dance the same steps most of the time, with an occasional solo thrown in.

The use of grouping to distribute dance material has several advantages. Each group member needs to learn and perfect only his own sets of twenty-four, thirty-two, or sixty-four counts, rather than an entire dance number. Grouping adds constant visual variation and provides novelty for the viewers, because even if the same step is being repeated, the total dance number is being delivered by different participants and in various formations.

Diversity in the show can also be supplied by using more than one group at a time, or by having several groups simultaneously doing different dances which coordinate into one large pattern. Changes in grouping can help to illustrate changes in the music, where new keys and themes herald new appearances of the performers. The use of groups allows the unison work, when it does take place, to have greater impact and stronger emotional effect when "all join in."

Working as groups, the performers can carry the audience's focus in different spatial directions. One group traveling from stage right to stage left, followed by another group on stage right moving from upstage to downstage, will draw the audience's attention to the new playing area. This scheme is useful for designing movement patterns, as well as for achieving a *quick cutting* effect. Quick cutting, a term taken from film directing, is a technique by which one shot or episode is instantly replaced by another. When quick cutting is used in conjunction with lighting, audience focus can be abruptly transferred from one area of the stage to another, generating visual excitement or adding a sense of episodic progression. Grouping can also be used to distract the audience in order to cover up a change of props, or to set other performers in place for the next scene of action.

One important rule should always be kept in mind: the larger the group, the less intricate its movements should be. This applies whether the performers are dancing alone or playing off the steps of another group. In the latter case, complementary patterns executed simultaneously will show both groups off, just as in vocal counterpoint, where two songs are sung at the same time and the melody of one fits into the pattern of the other song. The complementary dance material will only work well, however, if the movements are kept uncomplicated; if the routines are too involved and the dancers are not *exactly* on their counts, the result is an indistinguishable mess.

The choreographer must figure out which dancers, chorus people, and principals are available for the various sections of a given dance number. He must determine how many dancers, male and female, there are; how many people, male and female, are in the chorus; which principals, or leading characters, should be involved, as indicated by the script; and which other principals could plausibly be added to the number. Principals will always draw attention to themselves when they are involved in an ensemble piece, because the audience is more familiar with them and recognizes them as distinct personalities. The participation of the principals can make a statement about them, add coloration to the scene, or further their characters' development, so the choreography chosen for principals must be appropriate to their audience-accepted traits.

Imagination must be coupled with the abilities of the performers to determine which sections of the number will lend themselves to what types of dance steps and which dancers. The choreographer now marks the grouping divisions in the score, adding to his markings for counts, blocks, themes, and moments. The decisions as to who will perform which sections and blocks should be added lightly in pencil to allow for last-minute changes.

Let's go back to the "Farmer Dance" in *Oklahoma!* for an example of how to create a dance structure. (Note: this dance version is not based on the original DeMille choreography, but was developed in a community theater production.)

BLOCK	COUNTS	WHO DANCES
Introduction	16	all get in place
A	32	three couples
B	32	three men
C	16	Mr. Carnes
D	32	one couple
E	32	trio (2 girls & Will)
F	32	all dance
G	32	trio (2 boys & Annie)
H	26	all dance
I	24	Will and Annie
J	16	all sing and finish

Now that the choreographer has assigned a set of dancers to each musical section, the next step is creating steps for them. What kind of movement is suggested by the themes themselves and their musical treatment? General feelings can be sketched out, indicating ideas of the steps to be used at different times. While these steps are being specified, however, the floor plan must be worked out, showing *where* the various sections will be performed on stage and in what *directions* the dancers will travel.

FLOOR PLANNING

Where do the dancers go, and when? How do they get to their next positions? The *floor plan* is a step-by-step mapping-out of these travel patterns. Enough time must be allowed for the dancers to get to where they are supposed to be, prepare themselves, and perform. Keep in mind that a dancer cannot cross a stage in three beats or steps. The choreographer must make sure that a dancer can re-enter the stage where and when he is needed, both in terms of time and space. Did his previous combination end on the other side of the stage? When and where is his next appearance? Are any dancers being used in two or more groups consecutively? Is such a plan humanly possible?

One group must be able to clear the area where the next group will have to travel and be seen. One group cannot end their route where another must begin because people will tend to block each other. *Sightlines* must be observed: the action must be visible and not blocked by the angle of the audience's seats or other performers' placement on stage. A clear floor plan gives each group its own direction and goal of travel, and will prevent later traffic jams once rehearsals are under way.

There are nine basic divisions of the performance stage which are universally accepted in Western theater. "Stage right" and "stage left" refer to the actor as he faces the audience, that is, to the *actor*'s right and left. The front of the stage closest to the audience is referred to as "downstage," while the rear of the stage area is called "upstage." The terms "downstage" and "upstage" came into being back in the days when the seats of theaters were all on one level on the auditorium floor. To afford maximum visibility, the stage was tilted with its furthest side highest. This set-up was also called a "raked" stage. The raised side became "upstage," while the lower edge facing the audience became "downstage." Upstage, downstage, stage right, stage left, and center stage are combined into the scheme shown on page 81.

In scripts and general usage, "R" stands for right, "L" for left, "U" for up, "D" for down, and "C" for center. These initials are then combined to become SR (stage right), SL (stage left), DC (down center), UC (up center), UL (up left), and UR (up right).

While these are the labels for the most commonly used stage directions, there are also "house" designations which identify the stage areas as seen from the audience's point of

UP RIGHT	UP CENTER	UP LEFT
STAGE RIGHT	CENTER	STAGE LEFT
DOWN RIGHT	DOWN CENTER	DOWN LEFT

AUDIENCE

view. "Upstage" and "downstage" remain the same, but "stage right" becomes "house left" and "stage left" becomes "house right."

Some positions on stage are undoubtedly stronger or weaker than others. Different directions of travel will have different effects on the audience. Groups can take on various dynamics and contrasts, depending upon their placement onstage. Books on general choreographic elements usually discuss these variables in terms of design and dramatic focus. Of course, performers' positions, travel directions, and groupings must be constantly varied to remain effective.

Floor planning begins by making sketches of the plans on paper. Knowing the number of the performers and their individual abilities, the choreographer should assign the individuals to prospective groups, at least on temporary lists—the ultimate use of a performer will depend on his ability to handle the choreographic material once it is created. A floor plan of the set design will also be helpful in seeing where the stage props will be located during the dance sequence.

The choreographer needs to remember that not all movements are locomotive. Much choreography will be devised to be danced in one place with little or no directional travel at all, especially in ensemble unison work, where the stage is full of active bodies.

Use a code system of whatever symbols you wish, such as "A"'s and "B"'s, or "x"'s and "o"'s, for mapping the floor plan, drawing arrows to indicate the direction of the traveling party or parties. Keep in mind that the floor plan should represent an "aerial view" of the stage. Draw a series of sketches to plot the routes of travel and keep track of their sequence. The first sketch will show where the primary performers begin; use an arrow to indicate the part of the stage to which the group is moving, and underline the symbol to show the group's destination. For the next sketch, draw new arrows to represent either the first group's next travel patterns or the route of a new group. This paper-sketch process forces the choreographer to build the dance number piece by piece and makes him decide what to do with a group once it has finished its combinations and is no longer the focal point. Do these performers stay in the performing space, exit the stage, or join the onstage spectators? *Where* do they go? Are they needed to reappear in the same dance number from a different location? How do they get to their next position?

Through continuous sketches, the choreographer proceeds through the dance number. The sketches should be labeled in numerical or alphabetical order, but should also include the measure numbers from the score which coincide with the stages of movement, indicating at what point movement is begun and when movement is completed. For general group design, a simplistic sequence might look something like the diagrams on page 83.

In this sequence, as each group clears the central performing area, another group enters to replace it.

The three sketches on page 84 represent a segment of the number in which two groups travel simultaneously. Group A moves down left and down right; then Group B dances down center, as Group A dances up right and up left. The third sketch shows the final positions of both groups relative to each other.

Floor planning can also help solve the intricacies of travel placements when symbols like "x" and "o" are used to represent individual performers, as in the diagrams on page 85.

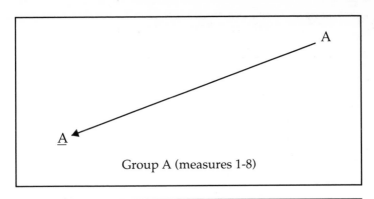

Group A (measures 1-8)

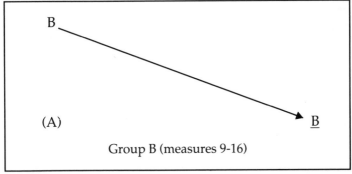

(A)

Group B (measures 9-16)

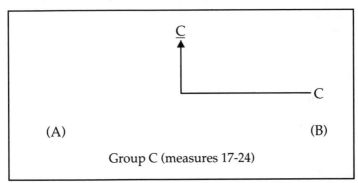

(A)   (B)

Group C (measures 17-24)

(C)

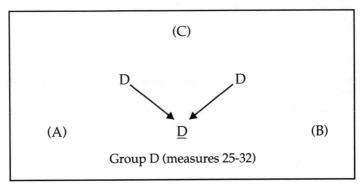

(A)   D   (B)

Group D (measures 25-32)

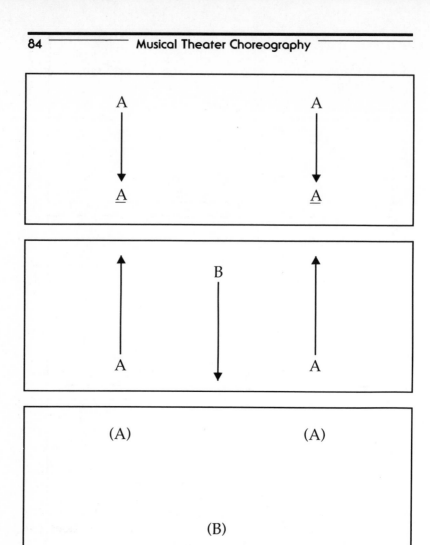

RISING ENERGY AND CLIMAXES

Now that the choreographer has marked the dance number's music, designed grouping patterns, and outlined a tentative floor plan, he must consider creating the accelerating power which results in the climax of the piece. Indeed, all the ingenious grouping patterns and routines would not mean much if there was no sense of advancement within them, if the musical number only seemed to plateau. To sustain audience

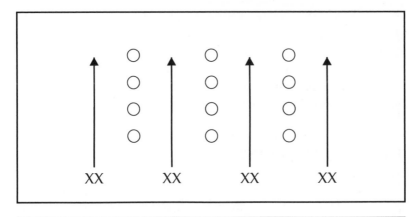

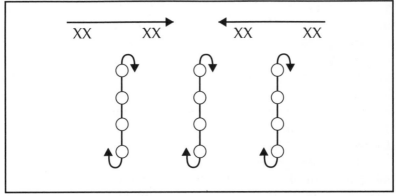

involvement, there must be a feeling that the number is going somewhere, that there is an emotional climb. How does one make a dance number "build" to a climax?

One way is through the music, with devices like accelerated tempo, heightened pitch, increase in volume or orchestration, and prolonged tension leading to a resolved chordal release. Another method is through juggling various visual elements of staging: increasing the number of people onstage, expanding the space being used, using larger movements, accelerating the speed of movements, or suddenly shifting from group dances to unison work.

Wedding the music to the choreography is the most effective way of creating the climax. The music and the action can build together, the music can remain constant while the action builds, or the music can build while the action plateaus. Keep in mind that the action cannot seem to build if the music is declining in its statement. As mentioned earlier, between action and music, the music will tend to override whatever is happening onstage. The only exception to this rule occurs when the music recedes *after* the climax of the piece has been reached, unwinding as part of the dénouement.

BEGINNINGS AND ENDINGS

There are a number of considerations in starting a musical number. The choreographer must determine whether the scene or musical number opens in a freeze (tableau) when the lights come up; whether the plotted movement of a scene transforms into stylization for a musical number; and whether one segment of the number calls for the appearance of new performers, or the disappearance of people from the segment before. There may be a combination of these ingredients, such as staging chorus members to stroll onstage into the setting and then join in the musical segment, going from natural movements to stylized dance movements.

If the performers are already onstage, the choreographer must ask himself: Where on the stage are the characters and chorus members at the commencement of the number and during its various blocks? Does a song come before the dance? If so, who is involved? Does the number arise from the blocking of a scene? What are the people doing, and what *have* they been doing, when the number begins?

However these questions are handled, the issue of plausibility must always be considered. Can the audience accept the premise for an ensemble's involvement in the staging? Is the chorus singing and dancing because they are caught up in the mood of the moment, or is their participation dramatically structured around a specific situation, such as when one character is teaching the others how to execute the song or dance? Unless purposely exaggerated, as in a satirical motif, the participation of groups of people in stage business should never call attention to itself. A musical number in a show, or the whole show itself, can be ruined by a ridiculous scene where everyone suddenly plunges full steam into a dance number without any apparent motivation.

The close of a dance number is just as important to the choreographer as is the opening of the number. Here are some issues for the choreographer to consider: Who should remain onstage? Are there gradual exits by chorus members, for a diminishing or fading-out effect? Does the dramatic action of the surrounding scene resume after the completion of the musical segment? If so, where do the participants need to be onstage?

How the music ends is also an important point to consider. The music can sometimes discourage applause by either going right into scenic underscoring music—forcing an immediate return to dramatic action—or right into another musical segment. For example, in *West Side Story*, neither the mammoth "Dance at the Gym" nor the stirring "I Have a Love/A Boy Like That" duet can receive audience applause because of the way that they end, or rather, do not end. The "Gym" sequence is interrupted by stage action and the accompaniment of the song(s) leads directly into underscoring and dialogue.

7 CHOOSING THE STEPS

B y this point, the choreographer has familiarized himself with the script and the score, dividing the music into a system of counts, blocks, themes, and moments. He has created a floor plan which details the dance movements for the musical number. Before he can get to the "meat" of the choreography—selecting the steps to use for the dances—he must consider additional elements which will affect the shape and impact of his work: dramatic validity, the design of the dance, and the physical abilities of the dancers.

In choosing the proper steps for a dance number, the choreographer uses *dramatic validity* as a means of determining which steps, when coupled with the music, will most clearly convey the feeling of a scripted situation. Dances appear in the "world of the show" for a reason, so what elements in the plot "cause" the dancing, how the movements are executed, and how they conclude are all weighty considerations.

Whatever critical information is to be conveyed to the audience will be so noted in the script and the score. These notations will, of course, help the choreographer devise a visual rendition of a particular incident, and even when these notations offer only the vaguest or skimpiest descriptions of what is going on, the choreographer can still get a general idea of how to create a progression of events to achieve the required result.

Yet more importantly, since it is the emotional state of the characters that accounts for almost all of the dancing onstage, dramatic validity also means exploring how someone with particular character traits, and in a specific setting, would express the emotional state indicated by the script. Anyone dancing must communicate within the framework of the social restrictions and personal qualities that lend a unique flavor to each character. In depicting emotion, a line must be trod between the universality of certain movements and the moral climate of the production's setting. It is the choreographer's sensitivity to the "world of the show" that makes the difference between acceptable choreography and the raw outpouring of steps which do not refer to any time or place.

Choreography is actually a series of pictures, both moving and still, from one transition to another, so the *design of the dance* will give the piece an overall style and "look." This design encompasses the use of the body in terms of its lines, and the patterns formed by groups of bodies from the audience's point of view.

The choreographer must think of the dancers' bodies as elements of drama seen through a visual design. How are the dancers' bodies to be utilized to enhance the stage drama? Will different sides be used, the back be used, or will the performers always face front? Will the dancers serve as props or structures periodically, thereby relinquishing their status as individual personalities?

Spatial patterns can be defined as "how the movement cuts through the air." Is a dancer's body traveling as a whole from one place to another? Is only a part of the dancer's body, such as an arm or leg, changing its placement? Whether a dancer's body in whole or in part is moving, a path will be traced in space as the dancer moves from one point to another until it reaches its destination. These patterns of movement define the style and design of the piece.

Design of the dance piece also means considering how many dancers are moving at the same time. Are there to be groupings or only unison work? Will different fractions of the ensemble dance in turn or will more than one division move at the same time? Is there to be an alternating structure where one group holds still while another group is active, and vice versa? Are any "progressive" movements to be included, where an action is performed by individuals consecutively in sequence? Examples of progressive movements would be a waterfall effect, or a dance pattern in which the original participants automatically supply new movements that are imitated by others.

Unless the choreographer is working with a varied group of trained, sensitive, and versatile dancers, the *physical abilities of the dancers* must be estimated as accurately as possible during the creation of the pieces. Different circumstances will set different conditions. A high-school or college production's youthful cast will be capable of more energetic and intricate output, even without previous training, than a production utilizing middle-aged members of a community accustomed to a sedentary life style.

Almost anyone can learn sequences of steps through repetition when they are correctly correlated with the performers' abilities. At all times, the steps must be kept simple and clear. "Simple" steps are those which are straightforward and free from complicating adjustments; "clear" steps are ones which the choreographer can explain effectively.

Many routines do not require extensive footwork; even the "ordinary" language of classical ballet is composed of relatively simplistic two- and three-part movements. In fact, the number of basic locomotions which can be accomplished by two feet is limited. The choreographic use of arms and hands will make major and minor statements, giving any dance routine its style and emotional flavor. In a group experiment, the choreographer may want to demonstrate identical combinations of steps and slowly add the movements of limbs to illustrate how moods and acting dynamics change with the use of different body parts.

More important than the dramatic validity of the steps, the design of the dance, and the physical abilities of the performers is the accessibility of the choreography. All the dance movements must be within the performers' reach. Because of their physical limitations, lack of a trained eye for imitative technique, and the all-too-common lack of mirrors in a nonprofessional environment, the dancers are that much more dependent upon the choreographer's capacity to observe and critique, since they cannot recognize their own flaws. The choreographer is simultaneously the only model and only source of correction.

CREATING THE DANCE STEPS

All dances are combinations of set poses, steps, and transitions. The term *set poses* not only applies to frozen postures held for a period of time, but also signifies the fact that for choreography to remain constant and repeatable, the dancers must be in certain positions at certain assigned times, that is, on exact counts. Even though the dancers are moving continuously, a step is, in reality, made up of a series of poses, the dancers passing from one pose to the next to create the illusion of a step. If a photograph were to be taken at any time during the execution of a dance, that particular moment (and pose of the step) would be captured apart from the completed pattern. *Steps,* then, are movements by which dancers go from one pose to another. *Transitions* are the movements between certain poses which cannot be pinned down to distinct counts, yet which must progress at a given speed for the poses to occur when needed. The beginning and ending poses can be matched to counts, but the time to get from one pose to the other will be phrased according to the time necessary for the movement to meet its counts.

Types of Steps and Variations

Ballet, jazz, tap, and various ethnic styles of dance all have specific vocabularies for the kinds of steps they use. The types of steps in musicals can generally be categorized according to their function. *Sterile dance steps* do not require any dramatic or emotional involvement to perform. *Dramatic combination steps* fit into the plot structure by expressing some suitable emotion, and are standard steps colored by intention. *Dramatic non-combination steps* represent a cross between gesture and dance movements; they are stylized and created for expressive reasons. *Straight mimed gestures,* movements which are close examples of realism, literally signify a particular act or statement. *Steps of "being"* establish a character or mood, but with no direct reference to the plot, and merely show the audience what a character is like or how he is feeling.

Various styles of dance and movement have established unique vocabularies that reflect their presentation, or have created subdivisions of fundamental movements, such as the additional beatings of the feet in ballet, or the multiple sounds in tap. However, there are really only eight means of conveying the body on two feet: walking (going from one foot to the other while maintaining constant contact with the floor); leaping (going from one foot to the other without constant floor contact); jumping (going from two feet, through the air, to two feet); hopping (going from one foot, through the air, to one foot); sliding (going from one place to another, while maintaining floor contact with the traveling foot); skipping (going from one foot to the other with a slide beat in between); and standing (going from one foot to two feet, or from two feet to one foot).

If a body is stationary and does not have to move around the stage, the feet and legs can be used freely and independently, allowing for the creation of new movements. As soon as the weight of the body is being moved from one place to another, however, the above list exhausts the options of movements. Of course, choreography can call for transference *not* on two feet, such as crawling about on all fours, rolling along with the full body, or other such movements. But standard dance vocabularies and common movements are based on these options of movement.

The arms and hands, as well as, to a slightly lesser degree, the head and body, are used to further refine the statement of the feet. Some foot patterns immediately designate a time or place, such as the Charleston, can-can, Highland Fling, minuet, or tango. All these steps are recognizable upon appearance, without the aid of additional signals. Some foot patterns depict only high or low energy levels until arm/hand placement and body angle are added to give them more character.

The very same steps can represent different national identities solely through different use of arms, hands, and head. Again, every step must be adapted and made appropriate to the specific instance of the show. The "Latin" style called for in *West Side Story,* the "Mu-Cha-Cha" from *Bells Are Ringing,* the "Tango" in *The Boyfriend,* or the "Havana" sequence in *Guys and Dolls* make for all different times, places, moods, tensions, and statements. Although all these scenes utilize the "Latin" steps, the performers should execute them in a manner specific to the motif.

Unique steps can also be created for a special context. For example, the "Crapshooters' Dance" from *Guys and Dolls* is, by definition, a danced session of shooting craps. This scene focuses on a central point on the floor where the dice are being rolled, and on the tension of the men anticipating the results. To bring these two elements together, the choreographer must consider the different ways that the shaking, rolling, and throwing of the dice can be given stylized movements, as well as how to express the men's excitement and suspense. The choreographer can sense that there is going to be some *floor-work,* that is, dance combinations which take place with the body on the floor. The players may leap in the air with enthusiasm as they shake their dice, then hurl their torsos to the ground as they roll the cubes out, diving to the floor to see the outcome. (To spare a great deal of confusion and excess coordination, the dice themselves should merely be mimed, since they are so small that the audience could not see them anyway.)

Any step can be broken up and varied to sustain interest. Tempo, direction of the movement, height, level of stage, use of arms, focus of the performer, rhythm of the step in conjunction with the music, the footwork or emotional state and motivation of the characters—all these, and any number of other creative options, are up to the choreographer to shape and vary freely. A simple feat, such as walking around on a stage, can provide a wealth of material for holding a spectator's eye or capturing his imagination. Through gradual or abrupt transitions, the audience can remain continually involved as the character in question brings new aspects of himself to view.

But steps or situations will become boring if no development is apparent, or if no new factor is introduced. The major ingredient at work is that of *change,* either through a sense of progression or surprise. A steady sense of achievement can even become tedious without interruption: the obstacles are what the plot is all about. Audiences love to be surprised, but always within an acceptable context. If an unexpected event occurs, like a humorous *non sequitur,* the viewers should never have to scratch their heads trying to figure out the link between the situation and the additional movement.

Just as every step and gesture must be appropriate to the specific situation, so, too, variations on and diversions from these movements must fit in. In the quest for novelty, it is sometimes easy to come up with ideas and "bits" which seem funny and clever in rehearsal; but will they be truly effective in performance, or will their meanings be too hard for the audience to grasp? No diversion should prevent the audience from understanding the performer's movement.

Starting Points

How does one start to make up choreography? How is it created to accompany the music? There are different ways of beginning, depending upon individual preference, the type of job to be done, and the choreographic inspiration that finds itself by dint of concentration. Sometimes it seems easier to work from the inside, bringing feelings to the surface and representing them. Sometimes it is more relevant to begin with an external appearance and work toward a cohesive picture.

These are the two basic methods of approaching choreography: working internally or externally. A choreographer working *internally* will create the steps by executing them himself through feeling and motivation, then refining them by analyzing the visual components, either by looking in the mirror or by teaching them to someone else and reshaping the steps on the dancer's body. When creating *externally,* visual display is all that is considered. All dance movements are constructed in such a way as to transmit an illusion of the appropriate feeling. Sooner or later, every choreographer must make use of both procedures.

If a specific dance style is being copied or emulated, selected poses or movements might be chosen as the foundation upon which to build the work. This is one time when the choreographer's research will come into play, especially if photographs of an original production are being used. Of course, these frozen moments do not show all the stylized steps from one movement to another. If the choreographer has seen a production of the show or even a film version, he can cultivate his impressions into kernels of routines and positions. Another way to start is to work directly with the music. Listen to it carefully—what emotions does it evoke? Does it have a feeling of movement? Does it swirl upwards, pound as a march, or flow lyrically? Finally, you can begin with the stereotypical steps known to be applicable to the situation, and either assemble them into new routines or use them as a basis for exploration—for example, haul out the Charleston or Black Bottom for building a '20s routine.

Thematic Steps and Variations

A basic mistake of novice choreographers is the confusion between the use of thematic steps and the repeating of whole combinations. *Thematic steps* are just what the name implies —individual steps of specific design which are used to create variations that possess a common bond. A thematic step works like a musical theme: it is stated and, once it is established, is varied or departed from to provide constant interest.

With the thematic step as the structural base, the choreographer develops a variation by having the dancer do the same step but change the angle or direction of its delivery, or by altering the step so that it becomes a variation on itself. In the latter case, there must be some similarity between the original and the offshoot, or the variation will look like new subject matter. When repeated in a thematic move, the steps, both preceding and following the move, must be checked to ensure that the desired look will be achieved.

Steps and routines may be repeated throughout a piece with no new varying element, if these instances are not too close together in time. In fact, it is sometimes wise to periodically return to the theme steps for stability and consistency. Immediate repetition of an exact step or even whole combinations can be acceptable and not necessarily boring.

There is, for example, the classic *triple-repeat-and-break pattern*, in which a step, or set of steps, is repeated three times in succession, either identically or alternatingly from side to side. Instead of a fourth repeat, however, a different step or break is included for the ending which will complete the musical phrase and match the musical resolution. This pattern is especially used in tap-dance combinations where, for instance, a time step is repeated three times and followed by a break, which varies yet completes the rhythm pattern. Generally, it is a good practice not to exceed three or four successive repeats of any step by one group at one time, in order not to lose audience interest. A combination may be repeated identically, if performed by different groups, though even then, some additional variation, at least at the end of each set, would help.

FEEDBACK

As the steps and movements begin to crystallize into dance routines, the choreographer needs to know if his intentions are coming across clearly. Who should see and judge the choreographer's output? Some people will see the choreography by virtue of mere proximity—the rehearsal pianist, performers, and other staff members. It is the choreographer's right to insist upon *closed rehearsal,* where no one is present except those who are involved in the work itself. Such a rehearsal will always help to reduce the choreographer's and the performers' tensions, promote creativity, and reduce the fear of experimentation. It will also minimize distractions.

When the the choreographer feels that the time is right for some feedback, there is the question of who will be the first viewers. Whose opinions does the choreographer trust in terms of honesty and accuracy? What is his relationship to this person? He will get quite a different critique from his mother or mate, who thinks he can do no wrong, as opposed to an artistic rival who never liked him anyway. Trust is also a primary concern. The discretion of this select audience must be assured, so that they will not share their knowledge or opinion with the public or the production company members and generate either negative feelings or complacency.

How many opinions should one get? Generally, a cross-section of viewers is necessary to some degree to gain perspective on the relative merit and acceptability of the work. One should not endlessly solicit opinion-seeking approval, nor consider each critique as absolute truth. One can get an accurate idea of the material's effectiveness by talking to two to four well-chosen viewers.

Besides honesty, accuracy, and trust, a viewer's knowledgeability about what he is seeing is an important consideration. But sometimes this perspective is a desirable quality, sometimes not. A viewing of his work by people with theatrical or dance backgrounds is valuable to the choreographer for an appraisal of the quality of his contribution to the field. If a knowledgeable person has ever seen other productions featuring the choreographer's work, that person can help to gauge the new project artistically and technically. However, it is also beneficial for a person *without* extensive background in theater or dance to contribute opinions. Such a viewer will have a better grasp of the true clarity of the work and will more accurately represent the majority of the house audience. Therefore, to evaluate his work both artistically and commercially, it is a good idea for the choreographer to receive comments on both levels.

It is only fair that the director see your output to know what material is developing in his production. However, if the director sees a piece prematurely, he may only worry or demand changes which may be unfounded because the actual content of the work is not yet clear.

When should a work be viewed for feedback? How early in its development? Again, there are several facets of the work-in-progress to consider. Is the dance piece complete? How clean are the dance routines? Are the mime and dramatic portions explicit? Will there be enough rehearsal time for making major changes or rectifying a problem by opening night?

There is a first stage for possible viewing—early in rehearsals, when all the pieces of the number, such as the groupings and sections, have been assigned but still require corrections, when the dancers are progressing from working strictly with counts to working with the music. A work should never be shown when segments are untaught or people are missing. If the piece is incomplete, a fair appraisal cannot be made.

Verbally describing the work to the viewer must be considered cheating, because the work is supposed to be self-explanatory at all times through its images and the music. (The only exception to this would be describing those props or pieces of scenery that will significantly affect the movements.) After all, no one will be filling the audience members in on what *they* are supposed to be seeing.

How to deal with feedback about the structure of a dance number or the steps themselves is up to the individual. To weigh the validity of a judgment, the choreographer must consider its source—to put it bluntly, whether the person knows what he is talking about. If the suggestions are justified, the next question to answer is how these changes can be implemented with the least trauma to the performers.

8 COSTUMES, SCENERY, PROPS, AND LIGHTING

W e will now explore the relationship of the costumes, scenery, props, and lighting to the choreographer's work. All of these elements will influence the final result, so it is vital to work with them as early as possible to establish the limits of potential movement.

COSTUMES

No other factor will affect the dances as directly as the costuming. Costumes can enhance or impede movement; they can also be used as part of the choreography in specific steps, or as a stylistic feature of the overall dance piece.

The flow of fabric and use of extended pieces, such as sleeves, trains, hats, flounces, hoop skirts, and veils, all carry with them movement of their own. If planned into the design of the choreography, these pieces can add fullness and specialty. If they are not properly planned for, the extended pieces will bring clumsiness and possible entanglement.

The costume designer and choreographer must consult with each other to establish what a dance number will entail before any rehearsal is begun, or designs made, by either party.

Just as the costumes can show off choreography, the dancing can help display the attributes of the garments. Both choreographer and costume designer must bear each other's work in mind during creation. Each must ask the other, before disastrous assumptions are made, "Can we do this?" and "Can you supply that?"

The Planning Process

Planning for the costumes begins with the primary production meeting, when the director explains the approach to the show as well as the physical confines of the theater facility and the budget. The choreographer and costume designer should soon meet separately from the group, at a time when the choreographer can share prospective dance patterns with the designer, and the costumer can render sketches of the projected work. The back-and-forth exchanges of information during the initial periods of creation will help the two to constantly refine each other's output.

The next stage comes when the designer offers the choreographer sample pieces of the costumes-to-be so that he can to see how the styles match the dance steps. Costume design for dance is a very different matter from creating clothing for people who merely stand or walk around. Balance, weight, flow, length, and even texture take on new importance. These are some of the questions for discussion: What kind of undergarments will the dancers be wearing? Are the fabrics such that the over- and under-layers will slide across each other when grasped, making lifts impossible? Is the hem so deep that it can be stepped into, possibly causing a fall? What is the skirt length, and will the foot get caught during a kick or when performing an attitude? Does the material fall into place after a movement or does it bunch up? Can the partners get near each other with their hats on? Will the sleeves allow the arms to move as planned? Will the crotches permit the vital flexibility of the hips and legs?

These types of questions must all be answered for the dance to work in both rehearsals and performance. The specifics, of course, will depend upon the exact costume and choreography. In one instance, I worked on a production where the dancing girls' skirts were designed to have the material gathered and bunched on one side or the other, and they were constructed of heavy fabric. The resulting dresses were so off-balance that when the girls attempted to execute the pirouettes in the number, the dancers simply fell over.

Footwear

Footwear is the responsibility of the wardrobe department. While dancers will be wearing one type of shoe for rehearsals, the shoes used in performance can make or break the delivery of the steps. Whether soft jazz shoes, hard "character" shoes, ballet slippers, gymnastic slippers, or tap shoes, they must be properly broken in before the dancer faces the audience in them. If the shoes are stiff, with the bottoms not worn down where they need to be, the dancer might as well be walking a tightrope. Contact with the floor must feel absolutely secure, and the shoes should feel pliable and exist as an extension of the foot. Controllable qualities of traction, balance, and flexibility should be determined *before* the live performance.

Facsimiles

Facsimiles of important costume pieces should be used in rehearsal as soon as the performers are secure with the steps, so that they can incorporate into the total movement the feel and balance of the costumes. Using the facsimiles also gives the choreographer a chance to see how the projected costume plans are working, and allows him to experiment with, and draw inspiration from, the movement qualities of the garments.

Accessories which will severely inhibit movement should be considered only with careful planning or avoided altogether, for even the wind resistance of a small article can slow execution and hamper turns. Wigs and hats must be securely fastened and checked for imbalances and whipping strands. I can recall a production where the dancers were required to have short pigtails, which smacked them squarely in the eyes when they turned. Eventually, the solution was to attach the pigtails to the dancers' shoulders with Velcro.

SCENERY

The scenery will dictate the size and shape of the playing areas as well as the usable set pieces: entrances, exits, windows, platforms, or stairs. The choreographer must know the exact limitations, obstructions, and availabilities of scenery for each number to be staged.

In addition to foreseeing what will be shaping the available space onstage, the choreographer must plan to answer these questions about the *offstage* area: Is there room for an ensemble backstage where needed? When groups must enter or exit *en masse*, will there be bottlenecks or traffic jams because of confinement? Can a performer exit off one side of the stage and re-enter from the other side; is there a backstage crossover? Can centrally placed, freestanding units like steps and platforms be "escaped" from? Where are the "escape" stairs to get the performers off the platform into the backstage area?

The Planning Process

As with planning for costumes, working with the scenery starts with the general production meetings, followed by a series of private consultations with the props manager to correlate the work of the choreographer with that of the props departments. Both the choreographer and the set designer should discuss the layout of the scenery *before* any dance movements are attempted. A scaled ground plan must be available for the choreographer's reference, showing the floor size, the shape of the space, and its accessibilities. All this information is essential to the choreographer in order to compute time allowances for steps crossing these areas and the placement of crowds. The design plans should indicate how much room there will be for dancing, and include critical elements like major stage props, set pieces used for concealing performers, entrances and exits, and open space. Until all these elements are identified, the choreographer cannot begin creating the physical structure of a dance number.

Once the scenic design is fairly firm, the choreographer can begin to experiment. Over time, inspiration, or the way a dance sequence is developing, may require altering the scenic designer's initial set-up, in which case the choreographer should notify the designer as soon as possible.

Scenery in the Rehearsal Area

For rehearsals, the areas designated for sets, entrances, exits, and important stage props should be measured and accurately taped out on the rehearsal floor. (More on this in Chapter 11.) These tape marks, delineating the playing area, must not be approached closer than three feet. Bear in mind that amateur performers tend to deal with invisible walls by going right up to the lines, so keep them from getting too close. After all, the lines represent future walls, barriers, or obstructions, and one does not come face-to-face with, or pass a gesturing arm through, most walls.

Once the performers get onstage, there will inevitably be a feeling that the playing area has been reduced from the rehearsal situation, even if the areas were accurately taped out. This feeling of restriction happens because one can no longer go right up to those drawn lines, and because the scope of vision is intruded upon by the collection of set pieces, especially if one has become accustomed to rehearsing in an open space.

PROPS

There are two major types of props: hand props and stage props. Props, like costumes and set pieces, usually do not have to be incorporated extensively into a dance number, unless the script calls for them. On the other hand, the choreographer may come to ask, why not use these props? Do they work naturally within the number? Can particular props create unity by linking the number to other parts of the show? Since various props are going to be available, the choreographer should feel free to use them when appropriate.

Stage Props

Stage props are those freestanding pieces normally not carried by hand, and usually considered part of the scenery. Examples of stage props include furniture, bridges, trees, boulders, and fountains. Of course, every stage prop should be included in the set designer's floor plan. These props are, however, more flexible in positioning than constructed scenery. During rehearsals, the stage props should be approximated with something of similar size, shape, and function. Even if these props are not directly used in the acting or dancing, they still represent obstructions which must be worked around.

The choreographer should discuss with the designer whether a piece is to be "practical" (usable) and, if it is, *how* it is to be used. For example, is the boulder strong enough for people to stand on or is it only a facsimile made of papier-mâché? Both "boulders" may be hollow for portability, but only one is strong enough to withstand additional weight. Test the piece for strength and balance before anyone attempts to use the piece in the context of the number. Depending upon the precariousness of the movement to be executed, spotters should be on hand for safety reasons, until the performance is successfully achieved.

Hand Props

Hand props, logically enough, are articles which are carried by hand, whether ornamental, symbolic, or practical. As part of his homework, the choreographer should explore using any props that would naturally lend themselves to a given character, setting, or style of a dance number.

If an object seems appropriate, a sample of the item should be obtained and experimented with in order to judge how it works and whether it has choreographic possibilities. The use of these props can provide novelty, humor, thematic steps, and thrills; whole pieces of choreography can even be built around key props. By cleverly managing, and finding new uses for, ordinary props, the choreographer can create a constantly entertaining performance.

Almost anything that can be held in the hand can become an important hand prop, if properly treated. Common dance props, besides the classic hat and cane, would include: trays (loaded or unloaded), chairs, umbrellas, baskets, ropes, swords, guns, whips, brooms, mops, and flowers. The list of hand props is endless. Fred Astaire was famous for ingeniously partnering with inanimate objects, such as a walking cane.

As with costume pieces, approximations of the hand props to be used in performance must be worked with in rehearsals as soon as steps are established. Working with the props early on will enable the dancers to achieve dexterity and a sense of security with the objects.

LIGHTING

At its most basic level, lighting determines whether or not the performers will be seen. For the choreography, good lighting can truly be the frosting on the cake. With sufficient lighting equipment, the elaborations can be infinite. Lit areas can be small, large, or anywhere in-between. The light can be shaped, sharp, or given a fuzzy edge. Colors and shades literally run the spectrum from pure intense hues to muted and blended tones. The source of light, as well as the direction and angle of its beam, can be used for varied effects. Silhouettes and shadows bring contrasts and complementary highlights. Some spatial effects have become standardized: strobes (though these can impair depth-and-speed perception in the performers), scrims, and stencils.

Moods are definitely set by the color, shape, and changes of lighting during the scenes and sequences. Emotional qualities can be represented or reinforced as well. Lighting can convey physical feelings, such as impressions of heat, warmth, cold, open space, or a cramped area. The frequency and intensity of mood-provoking elements will determine the stylistic framework of the dance piece—natural representation, abstract setting, stylized reality, or total stage fantasy.

The Planning Process

There are a number of lighting matters for the choreographer to consider. How does he want the steps to be seen, with regard to the lighting? (Dance sections to be done in silhouette, for example, require lighting that will be different from those dances that will be lit from front or side.) Will full stage lights be on all the time? Should limited areas be lit separately to allow for quick changes of focus, spontaneous appearances, and exits? (Small lights discretely placed on stage can help keep the performers from running all the way in and out of the wings.) A fundamental knowledge of the lighting facilities is also essential before the choreography can be realistically structured. The choreographer and the lighting designer need to discuss the following:

- approximate number of lamps, spotlights, and dimmers

- the special effects, as strobes or color filters

- the circuited areas already listed in the lighting plot

- instruments that can serve as "specials," that is, that can be reserved and focused for specific usage

- choice of colors

- desired moods

- stage areas related to the choreography

- lighting cues

By the technician's changing the lighting, either sharply or subtly, great dimension and variety can be added to the number. Not only can mood be shifted, but the audience's focus can be instantly redirected where desired.

All aspects of the lighting, from colors, intensities, and stage areas to special effects, should be thoroughly discussed prior to the technical rehearsal, which will include running through the lighting effects. At the technical rehearsal, all aspects of the lighting are seen and refined, and the changes are built into the lighting cues.

Lighting Cues

The lighting director and the choreographer must decide together how much time to allot for a given dance execution—an instant, slow eight counts, or a phrase of music—and whether the lighting cue should be conveyed visually, verbally, or musically. As far as dance numbers are concerned, the cues will have to be learned musically, if there is no verbalization involved in the performance. The placements of the cues should be notated in a copy of the piano score for the lighting designer, the stage manager, and the choreographer.

Can the stage manager, who calls the cues, read music? If not, can he learn the counts of the phrases the way the dancers do, so that he can follow along numerically by beats? Can the stage manager recognize key passages or changes of theme in the music when listening? Can he take a visual clue from action on stage? Some code must be worked out among the stage manager, lighting director, and choreographer so that the lighting cues occur at their appointed times. Otherwise, you will assuredly have times of "dancing in the dark."

9 BALLET, TAP DANCING, LIFTS, AND FIGHTS

Most musical comedies will call for certain areas of technical expertise, like previous training and an understanding of established dance vocabularies (ballet and tap), or experience with planning and rehearsing for safety (lifts and fights). When the much-revived musical classics were first presented, they were conceived by choreographers with extensive professional backgrounds. Coupled with this was the idea that each show had to impress the public as unique and had to make a name for itself. Dance was one of the methods used to achieve this end. The public never wants a rehash of old material, which is one reason why so many musical shows have failed; at the same time, however, venturing too far into the daring makes the audience uncomfortable. So, there is a thin line between stimulating and acceptable.

Some musicals call for limited use of a lift, fight scene, or solitary tap number. Other shows require established dance vocabularies as a general approach: Agnes DeMille's choreography, for example, was created on a balletic foundation. Whether choreographing one production or many, chances are good that knowledge of at least one or two of the areas covered in this chapter will provide useful background.

BALLET

A distinction must be made between "ballet" in musical comedy and technically precise ballet dancing. Classical ballet in its purest form represents a codified dance technique that has been handed down and refined over the last four hundred years. Though there are different schools of thought as to accentuation, they all spring from a common, firmly established root of principle.

In musical comedy, the inclusion of ballet has broadened its meaning of the term. Originally, almost any dramatic dance number was referred to as "ballet." This definition was eventually refined to mean an extended dance sequence of episodic structure with an internal plot of its own. The *dream ballet* is an example of this type of sequence. *The King and I*'s "The Small House of Uncle Thomas," for example, is titled as a "ballet," though it consists of Oriental movements which are the very antithesis of classical ballet—flexed feet and hands, angular poses—and totally abandons classical ballet vocabulary. In the end, this type of dance piece's contributions to the plot can range from indispensable to superfluous. Such "ballets" can exist merely to entertain the audience, though they are frequently used to make a statement as well. Possessing self-contained plots, these dance sequences can often stand alone, divorced from the parent work.

While the term "ballet" can be used loosely in musical comedy, classical ballet *steps* are standard in most shows. Classical ballet is the basis of all dance utilized today, supplying a universal vocabulary for the identification of steps. In musical comedy, the legs and feet often perform classical steps, while the arms and hands provide the style required by the show's production. It should be noted that the outstanding choreographers (Balanchine, DeMille, Robbins, and Kidd) came from strong classical ballet backgrounds. Initially, jazz was integrated as a commercial style in musical comedies. Therefore, the outstanding choreographers blended jazz with ballet in their works.

Classical ballet rarely prefigures in musical comedy in its pure form, unless the musical calls for such usage specifically, as in *Song of Norway, On Your Toes,* and *Look Ma, I'm Dancin'.* Pointe work outside of this realm can be used for novelty, rather than as strict balletic reference. The use of ballet for novelty's sake can be seen in the treatment of "The Heaven Hop" from the revival of *Anything Goes,* where the chorus-girl "angels" are classically perched. Some shows employ a classical style, using balletic steps and vocabulary while making adaptations. Agnes DeMille's primary musical comedy works were based on this approach. She combined ballet with stylized movement gestures in her choreography for Aaron Copland's ballet "Rodeo." She later developed cowboys who could perform ballet repertoire without looking "balletic" for *Oklahoma!,* and did similar work for the sailors in *Carousel.*

When ballet, or a close adaptation of it, is required, and the choreographer's knowledge of the field is limited or nil, a specialist can be brought in. In such a case, the choreographer should not blindly relinquish the dance numbers to this person, but should collaborate with him. The specialist's expertise in ballet may contribute to the vocabulary of steps, classical mime, floor planning, grouping patterns, and partnering, but the statement and substance of the material itself should still reflect the aesthetic approach of the resident choreographer. Thus, in such a collaborative effort, the choreographer of the production must maintain a certain degree of artistic control.

Classical ballet training is of continuous use as a choreographic tool, since all commercial dance used today is derived from ballet. This common foundation facilitates communication as well, allowing the steps to be identified with universally accepted labels. Good training lends an understanding to the basic construction and execution of a balletic movement—momentum, balance, center of gravity, transitions, and the sequence of parts of a movement. However, classical ballet training can be a detriment to creative musical comedy staging if it is the *only* training that the choreographer uses as a reference. Ballet is certainly a desirable background for a dancer to have, but ballet training must be supplemented by exposure to other dance styles for the dancer to attain the versatility and adaptability necessary for musical comedy.

It is not feasible for the choreographer to teach the dancers classical ballet technique in a limited amount of time.

In an amateur or semi-professional setting, if a prominently balletic style is required, either new dancers must be recruited, or some drastic alteration in the dance piece's style must be made. Even though flexibility and control can be increased in any performer through warm-up exercises and classes, inexperienced dancers are generally unable to conquer the rigors of authentic ballet techniques. However, adaptations of classical steps can often be learned when used in combinations with other dance styles.

TAP DANCING

Tap numbers hark back to those periods in history when tap dancing was a popular style. All tap dances are not automatically the same: chorus girls from the '30s danced differently from a man in the '40s, and his style would not be the same as a that of a bunch of dirt-kicking cowboys. Some shows contain a single tap number for variety (*Oklahoma!, Cabaret, Seesaw, No, No, Nanette, Funny Girl*), while other shows have tap numbers that give a total look to the piece and create a sense of locale (*George M, Dames at Sea, Forty-Second Street*). And some shows have no tap at all. It appears frequently enough, however, to necessitate knowledge of the field. Even if the tap idiom is not used directly, no choreographer can afford to close himself off to an entirely serviceable vocabulary and technique. One never knows when such knowledge will come in handy, even if only to add accent to non-tap works.

Tap Styles

Tap dancing is performed with metal plates attached to the heel and toe of the shoe so that a sound is produced when the shoes make contact with a hard surface. The rhythms and patterns produced by the striking of the feet in rapid succession form the dance. The lightest, cleanest sound is the most preferable—a "tap" or "tck" sound, as opposed to a more prolonged scraping. The lighter the metal plate, the lighter and cleaner the sound will be. (I recommend the Capezio brand

Tele-Tones.) Almost any leather-soled shoe can become a tap shoe—just add the taps!

Balance is often severely altered by the taps. Tap dances are performed with the body in a "pulled-up" position, with one's weight held constantly over the balls of the feet for optimum control. The heels are lowered only when the specific sound produced by the heel taps is desired. Taps can be curved on the bottom, as they are on the Tele-Tones brand, so that only the smallest amount of metal will hit the surface when struck. All these factors can play havoc with holding one's balance during the weight changes, travel patterns, and physical maneuvers of the choreography. Because the taps are very slippery, too, traction is greatly affected. Putting rubber over the sole of the shoe to fit around the tap has become standard procedure. Because of these considerations of balance and traction, turns and leaps have to be carefully choreographed and rehearsed.

Soft shoe is a type of tap routine performed in soft-bottom shoes. It is rarely used in contemporary musical comedy because, historically, the soft-shoe routine represents the era preceding the advent of metallic plates, and because the muted sound does not carry to a large audience. Yet without taps to present the traction and balance problems, more dance variations are easily possible.

Fake tap, a term of my own invention, is a drastically simplified version of the previous two dance forms. Both tap and soft shoe utilize standard vocabularies for sound patterns and choreographic elements; fake tap consists of combinations of steps in which the rhythmic sounds of the feet are accentuated and varied but do not follow traditional tap steps per se. This style can be used when no dancers with tap training are available, or when rhythmic sounds should supplement, rather than dominate, the choreography of a dance piece.

Choreographing Tap

Although a tap number is based on the rhythmic use of the feet, it is still a *dance* which, like any dance, needs to be visually and audibly varied and exciting. As a dance, the tap number requires the same structuring, grouping patterns, spatial designs of steps, and climaxes as does any other number. Too often, the dance elements will be sacrificed or merely passed over for the emphasis on sound and rhythm if the choreographer is hurriedly training novice performers. Even in such situations, the choreographer needs to remember that repeated audible patterns can actually be broken up easily by visual variations.

If the choreographer has no tap training, either a specialist can be brought in with whom to collaborate, or a simplified fake-tap number can be constructed. If there is only one tap number in the show, it can be assigned to a teacher or choreographer proficient in tap, with the understanding that it must fit into the framework of the production. In one respect, it is easier to collaborate on a tap than on a ballet number: balletic steps inherently possess strong interpretive value, whereas a tap number's main worth lies in its simple ability to entertain.

If the choreographer *is* familiar with tap, then technically correct tap dancing can be taught within a relatively short amount of time. ("Technically correct" means dancing with weight forward on the balls of the feet and the knees slightly bent, tapping out clear sounds.) Tap can usually be taught within two to three weeks. While the overall length of the practice allowance need not be long, excessive repetition and constant review is essential.

Tap demands perfect accuracy: everyone must be doing the same thing at the same time, so that it all sounds like one giant step. Because of the necessary precision and the speed that a tap number requires, it will take more time to slowly accelerate from the initial learning pace to the performance tempo. To produce results in such a compressed time slot, one must rehearse daily. Every first, third, and fifth days, introduce new steps and add to the material already mastered. Each second and fourth day should be used for review: run through the routine as a single piece, incorporating whatever was shown at the previous rehearsal and correcting mistakes. The most important consideration is the time spent in running the number over and over—give "muscle memory" a chance to set in, and slowly build up the speed.

Obviously, in choreographing tap routines for novice dancers, simplicity must be maintained, with the physical and mental saturation points of the performers kept in mind. Yet even elementary steps can be woven into fascinating combinations. Basic steps can be taught in blocks of patterns and then repeated or rearranged in those blocks. For example, you can direct the dancers to do blocks A-A-B-C-A. Be aware of the use of silence; a tap number, after all, is really divisions of silence, and need not generate a continual rat-a-tat-tat of sound to be effective.

The choreographer should set up a system of notating the tap steps, and should teach this system to the performers to give them an accurate guide to follow outside of company rehearsals. After learning the steps, each dancer makes his own set of notes, which is then checked by one of his fellow dancers. The form of notation must be precise: the three-line system found in Chapter 12 is probably the most helpful because it lists the name of the step, the foot with which it is executed, and the timing of the step.

One of the minor considerations in the use of tap concerns the wearing of the shoes during non-tap segments. The metal plates will make noise whenever someone wearing them walks on the stage, and there may be difficulty in masking the sound during the scene preceding the tap number, while people are entering or getting into place. The performer should practice walking on the balls of his feet, with only the sole of the shoe touching the floor, yet without appearing as though he is treading on a sheet of glass. After all, the last thing you want during a scene is a clattering metallic sound heralding the approach of a tap number.

LIFTS

The lift can always be counted on to provide an accent or climax when desired. The way that a dance partner is handled during the lift will also reflect the predominant male-female relationship of the show's time and place. Does he treat her roughly, respectfully, gracefully, or abruptly? Is she tossed around acrobatically, or simply helped to be lighter than air?

While the lift can be a valuable choreographic ingredient, adding tenderness or spice to a dance, it can also seem tacky or garish when misplaced or misused. I once saw a spinning shoulder-lift added to the Embassy Ball sequence in a community theater production of *My Fair Lady*. The lift disrupted the restrained, elegant, British upper-class mood of the scene.

Care must be taken to coordinate lifts with the music. A large, spectacular lift should match a climactic or dramatic musical moment, or one will detract from the other.

Types of Lifts

As with any form of choreography, lifts can be created and invented in any number of ways. There are classifications and types of lifts which represent those most frequently used, and which vary in terms of their being energized or non-energized.

Hip lifts are the easiest to accomplish because of the leverage and limited travel distance of the lifted body. Hip lifts can be sustained or immediately disengaged, depending upon the need of the situation. Using the man's hip as a fulcrum and target, the woman jumps onto it, while the male keeps his arm (the same arm as the hip) tightly wrapped around her waist, simultaneously pulling her up. He leans away from the hip supporting the woman, making it more accessible for her seat.

With *straight-up-and-down lifts*, the man's hands are on the woman's waist, the woman holding on to the man's wrists. Both dancers bend their knees and straighten their legs at the same time. She jumps directly up, the extension of the male's arms adding travel distance in the air. She can return to the ground or land in another position, such as sitting on his shoulder or hip, or falling into his arms. Her preparation and jump need not be as ordinary as described. The jump can be an *assemblé* or other choreographed step. This sort of lift is very difficult to sustain at its peak, calling for a full press on the part of the man. Because it is a quick nonstop movement, it will convey energy and exuberance.

In *traveling-through-the-air lifts*, the woman's body actually passes through the air. Often, these lifts can be circular motions, such as a windmill, where her body is turned 360 degrees, like a propeller. The woman may be thrown around the man's back and caught in the front, or she may do a simple somersault over his back. These lifts must be broken down into their individual parts and taught for timing and coordination. The use of momentum is the key factor in their execution.

Group-conveyance lifts most often engage two to four lifters, or possibly a crowd. The supported party (man or woman) is either transported to another place by being lifted into a series of positions, or simply raised, held, and lowered. A group lift must be rehearsed for group coordination and safety, and provides a nice "star" or center-of-attention focus for one performer.

With *from-person-to-person lifts,* the performer lifted is transferred from person to person, either in midair or with a transitional step in between. The from-person-to-person lift can be used as part of an ensemble routine where all the dancers change partners at once or, again, to give "star" focus to a solo performer.

Pas-de-deux movements are the slowly executed, graceful liftings or grounded, supported couplings of the dancers that are meant to be sustained, as used in a dance piece where a flowing quality is desired. Classically designed steps form the basis of these movements.

Lifting Basics

The choreographer can explore any number of possible combinations of bodily entwinement and discover lifts of his own, such as having the woman hanging by her legs around the man's neck, or having a performer thrown into the air in any conceivable position. Whatever lift does not strain a muscle can be predictably executed and, if effectively done, will succeed.

However, doing lifts *can* be quite dangerous—any slight error or miscalculation can result in serious and possibly permanent injury. A clear explanation of both the process and the final aim must be understood by the partners involved. Warming up is vital for both performers—legs, back, arms, shoulders, and neck.

The *man* should always have his legs spread in a moderate second or fourth position for a broad yet comfortable base of support. He must always remember to lift with the force coming from his legs, and not with his back. In any lift, both the man and the woman prepare for the movement by bending their knees, and straightening them during the lift itself. While the man must concentrate on his strength, momentum, and balance, the *woman* should be aware of her poses in the air, the direction of travel, and where and how to maneuver her body so that she exercises the proper flexibility, yet maintains consistent muscle tension. If she does not tense and hold her muscles to support themselves, the man can feel like he is carrying "dead weight."

An exact system of counts must be worked out and utilized to ensure proper coordination between partners, providing precise timing for anticipation, positioning, and placements. The lift itself consists of several components: steps providing the necessary momentum and leading into the bending of the knees for the execution, the knee-bend itself, the lift, the amount of time spent in the lifted position, and the dismount or transition out of the sequence. Again, all these designated movements must be made with distinct counts.

When devising the count pattern to find out how long the various stages of the lift require, one should verbalize a steady tempo, calling out "5-6-7-8" to set the beat and begin the sequence on the following count of "one." The counts can then be adjusted as needed to fit the accompanying musical phrase, depending upon the complexity of the movements.

Once the sequence of the lift itself is counted out as a complete unit, it must be inserted in the dance number. The lift will take place within the steps of the set choreography of a number, so adequate preparation must be arranged out of the steps of the preceding dance combination. The choreographer must make certain that for each performer involved in a lift, the correct foot is free, and that there is enough momentum; that the balance is correctly placed, with the participants positioned in correct relation to each other; and that the arms and hands necessary for connection are available. Sometimes the dance has to be altered to allow for the lift, or vice versa. It is a matter of which was created first, which is easier to adjust, or which makes the more valuable contribution.

Spotters must be used until the lift is safely mastered by the participants. The spotters must know how the lift sequence is supposed to operate, and must be able to anticipate

the directions of the maneuvers and forestall possible problems. They must be prepared to handle the weight of the lifted
party, either to catch or aid in momentum; they should not
interfere, but must be there instantly and reflexively if required. It is good practice, for safety's sake and for the learning of the performers, to put the lifting couples through their
movements in slow motion initially, using the spotters to bear
the full weight of the "liftee." In this way, all can orient themselves to the direction of the travel, the bodily movements,
and the hand and arm connections.

Technical matters must be considered as well. Is there
room enough on stage for the lifts? Or, for example, are twelve
men trying to swing their partners through the air while trying to avoid pillars on the set? Costumes can certainly interfere with rehearsed lifts. We have discussed some of the
obstacles the costumes can present in Chapter 8. For a brief
review, the choreographer should think about the following
questions: Does the flow of the costumes, or do any trailing
pieces of the costumes, get in the dancers' way? Are the tex-
tures suitable for the required movements? Do the costumes
slickly slide across each other, rendering the male's grip useless? How do the undergarments participate in the sequence?
Are they too noticeable? For example, I once saw a production
where a girl's tight skirt had two slits on each side, right up to
her hips. When she was tossed and spun in the air during a
technical rehearsal, the front and back portions of the skirt, as
divided by the slits, flipped straight up, revealing what no
man but her husband should have seen! In addition, the dress
lost any "look" its particular style was meant to have during
this specific lift. As with any other dance movements, bulki-
ness and balance must be regarded as potential problems during lifts.

FIGHTS

Musical comedies, as a rule, do not call for much sword- or
gun-fighting. What usually happens is that a free-for-all
breaks out, disrupting a scene. There are, of course, different
kinds of staged fights—realistically mounted ones, stylized

movements, fights with large groups, or fights between duos. The fights can be used as parts of scenes, parts of dance numbers, and as dance numbers themselves. As the "movement specialist," the choreographer is the one called upon to stage or aid in the assembling of these fight sequences.

In any fight where bystanders become participants, there is an action-reaction process which moves the event forward and magnifies an effect. If there is a small group, there is a give-and-return among a limited number of characters. In a larger fight, there is a "ripple-in-the-water" effect, beginning at a focused point and expanding as more and more people become involved. *How* the participants get involved, whom they respond to initially, and whom they, in turn, bring into the fray depends upon their relation to the catalyst of the primary aggressive act. However, almost every large fight will begin with two active members and then spread to include surrounding observers, usually accidentally. There are exceptions to this pattern, such as the moment when the Sharks in *West Side Story* simultaneously start a fray in reaction to the death of their leader, and the Jets immediately retaliate. Even in the example just cited, there is a collection of private combats, rather than a mob hysteria with a single focus.

As with any musical number, motivational and structural questions must be asked. Who is involved in the fight? Where are the characters at the onset? What physical or dramatic action precedes the beginning of the event? Is the fight set to music, thus calling for a choreographic-type structure synchronized to music? Where should the fight occur on stage for maximum effect? Is the length, pace, and sequence predetermined by the script or by the score? How does the fight scene end, that is, with what physical act? Does the action build toward a freeze, as found at the end of the farmer-cowman fight in *Oklahoma!*? Is there a focused action within the general melee, as in *Guys and Dolls,* where Sarah Brown is seen slugging it out in the midst of the brawl in Havana? Is whatever activity preceding the fight resumed afterwards? Will dialogue be used as a lead-in, or during the action?

A floor plan should be worked out beforehand to determine how the onstage action will progress. The primary moves, involving a few characters, will take up a large stage area as the fight builds and the active members are shoved about. The first participants move from place to place initiating activity, jostling or striking onstage observers. The size of the conflict grows, but less and less travel occurs as more and more people join in. Thus, the fight becomes progressively limited to fixed areas of the stage, especially as the number of smaller battles within the larger fight arises.

How does the choreographer get the fighters from place to place? Smaller fights can be devised as part of the choreographer's homework, staged to music which will help dictate the fight's structure. A large ensemble fight, springing from a smaller fight, should be created using the actual participants to develop proper dramatic progression and timing. In a large battle, the fighters are grouped into smaller conflicting units of two, three, or four people each. In a crowded brawl, the dramatic distinction must be clear to the actors as to who is fighting whom, even if not clearly noticeable to the audience. Each of these smaller groupings has a conflict and focus which relates to the overall picture. For example, in the fight that breaks out during *Oklahoma!*'s dance number "The Farmer and the Cowman," the farmer *versus* the cowman is the general theme, but each individual farmer-and-cowman unit has its own little on-the-spot conflict. In principle, every member of the ensemble is on one side or the other, whether they are physically fighting or not.

The involvement of everyone is what provides the necessary look of chaos—many different, seemingly uncoordinated brawls going on at once. The key word here is *seemingly* because, though the action looks uncoordinated, moves and positions must be assigned to ensure a varied look. People do not always fight standing up, nor do they use the same angles, punches, or moves. In a fight involving only one or two focuses, every action must be directed and choreographed, but in a larger brawl, where there seems to be no primary focus— or, if there is one, where it is masked by the mayhem—the actors can be given positions in terms of stage area and bodily placements (poses, levels and angles) to use for composing their own sequence of events.

If the choreographer wants a primary focus in the midst of the fight, he should keep that focus stage center or prominently downstage. He should not waste his more ingenious progressions on the fighters located far stage right, far stage left, or upstage. When action is distributed all over the stage, audience focus will naturally return to stage center, unless it is tracking a line of action which is traveling elsewhere. If there is no such through-line to pursue, stage center is where developments will be noticed, be they humorous, dramatic, or whatever.

Everyone in a fight scene is smart enough to avoid intentionally harming his partner. However, by overly concentrating on his own actions, a performer may not be paying attention to his surroundings. There must be a constant awareness of everyone within proximity, whether they are participants actively involved in their own fights, or bystanders. The performers should not trip over or crash into each other. The common accident of the "elbow pull-back" presents a good example. A performer is delivering the bogus punch. As he draws his elbow back to commit the blow, he hits someone behind him, usually at face level.

The performers must also take into account props, scenery, and other physicalities. When a production opens, the cast will not have worked on the sets for very long. When a fighter in a scene is thrown against a piece of scenery, either the set piece will give out or the actor will. A physical object on the stage can break, tear, or fall; or if it is stationary, hitting that object can very well knock an actor out cold. The latter experience actually happened in a tech-dress rehearsal of *West Side Story*, where the actor playing Bernardo got hauled backwards in the opening "Prologue" rumble, hit his head on some metal piping on the set, and was knocked unconscious.

Allowance must also be made for performance nerves. The extra adrenaline of audience exposure (especially opening night) can create new energy levels and subsequent carelessness. The performers do not realize they have more pep, and their perceptions are off. They will hit harder and move faster without realizing it. This phenomenon should be discussed with the company to help the performers be aware of these differences within themselves and each other.

All action must be cued for proper sequence. This cueing allows the fight to build at the proper pace and with dramatic validity. In dramatically-structured fights (i.e. those which are part of dramatic shows), visual and physical stimuli serve as the cueing devices. The visual instance for a performer would be stated as such: "When you see such-and-such happen, initiate your assigned action." The physical cue is even more direct: "When so-and-so is pushed into you, push him back." In this way, if everyone knows his cue, the fight will progress with the desired and natural effect.

In a fight which is coordinated with accompanying music, the actors can take their cues from musical counts as they would in a dance, along with using the obvious visual and physical cue methods. Yet the choreographer must make sure the actions sustain, and coordinate with, the musical statement. Unless the performers are given drastically stylized movements, actions and reactions should be expressed at natural speeds, yet fit into the count system and phrasing of the scoring.

The choreographer must also address the ever-essential issue of pacing. Characters need time for suitable reactions (literally called "reaction time"), as well as for thought processes that the audience can see. Remember, the viewers can only base their opinions and follow the progression of the story according to what externalizations they can recognize. If a character is supposed to formulate an idea or respond to input, whether physical or mental, the audience must be signaled that such an event is taking place.

This idea of signaling does not mean that every moment must be announced with fanfare, but it does mean that the staging and acting must take certain natural procedures into consideration. For example, an actor must see a prop on stage before he can logically use it. The absence of this nuance can insert humor where it does not belong: "How did he know the prop was there?" In a similar fashion, an actor must react to a situation before he will respond.

If the dramatic movements proceed without these specified moments of "digestion," the scene will seem needlessly artificial and probably run faster than the audience can comfortably follow. This is because the audience will naturally hold mental beats to supply *their own reaction time* to various situations. There is the alternate danger of the action proceeding too slowly if too much time is allotted between movements. These pacing balances must be discovered by the choreographer through experimentation and experience.

10 AUDITIONS AND CASTING

B efore we begin with the considerations and procedures regarding auditions and casting, two qualifications must be made clear. First, the information in this chapter applies to *dance auditions*, whereas testing singing and acting abilities is the responsibility of the music and stage directors, who have their own audition methods. Second, the material here is geared primarily to amateur choreographers.

THE CHOREOGRAPHER AND THE CANDIDATES

The audition will be the choreographer's first experience in working with others in a performing group. Until this time, he has done his research and experimented alone or with an assistant, and attended meetings with other members of the production staff.

Approaching a mass of strangers as a supposed expert or, at least, an authority on dance and movement, the novice choreographer may be tense. Remember, though, that the people who have come to audition are even more nervous. For them, dance auditions are even scarier than acting or singing auditions, for while the actor/singer can prepare ahead of time with the show's script and lyrics, the dancer cannot prepare himself for the choreographer's trial material. Therefore, clarity and patience in the teaching of an audition routine is a must.

The purpose of the dance audition is to see the capabilities of the potential cast members. Be ready with material which is representative of the style of the show yet also within the scope of the candidates' mental and physical abilities. Give the candidates steps being *considered* for the production, but which are not necessarily in a finished state. In fact, the choreographer's combinations should not be too solidified at this point in production, unless he has done this particular show before. He will most likely have to adapt the material to suit the *new* performers anyway. The routine can be structured to begin very simply and gradually become more complex as the steps progress. In this way, the choreographer can see when a prospective performer has reached his limits of execution or absorption, and he can have the candidate learn only to that point.

Setting a comfortable, constructive atmosphere, the choreographer must help the dancers grasp the material as quickly as possible, since speed is important—not only later in rehearsal, but at once—for giving all those auditioning equal time. But bear in mind that, because of the rushed time element and nervousness, the candidates may learn routines incorrectly at the audition. This can be a problem, because later, in rehearsal, the participants may fall back on their initial, flawed delivery. It is very hard to unlearn an ingrained physical action.

Each candidate should be evaluated according to the following criteria: basic comprehension; technical ability (any previous dance training); technical *potential*; speed of learning; grasp of dynamics (a feel for *how* the step should look); ability to understand and apply correction and direction; and attitude toward the work and toward others.

The importance of this latter quality cannot be overemphasized. Attitude can not only make or break a dancer's individual performance, but also severely affect the work of all others. Any production is truly a team effort, with everyone involved in the show striving toward a common goal; the only force propelling such an endeavor forward is the personal motivation of all concerned. Even a small amount of negativity can be dangerous to motivation. Because the choreographic task ahead will be rigorous, the choreographer should keep an eye out for the slightest sign of bad attitude, be it arrogance, self-indulgence, argumentativeness, disruptive behavior, or even simple lack of attention. Unfortunately, once the problem is discovered, it can be too late to cure, in which case dismissal, while an unpleasant task, is often the only solution. It is easier to work with untrained yet motivated people than with trained people who will not participate fully.

The choreographer is not at auditions to show off, intimidate the crowd, or be rude or condescending. He should not befuddle the candidates with dance jargon, technical terminology, or unclear explanations of steps. Always remember, particularly on the nonprofessional level, that everything in the show's production will be an educational experience for those involved. Give them a chance to learn. This is not the place to bolster one's ego by maintaining a facade of importance or remaining aloof, for the choreographer *needs* these people as much as they need him.

The audition requires dance steps that can be broken down efficiently into simple components. The choreographer should avoid any "tricks" or unnecessarily difficult steps; routines that require advanced technical skills (balletic beats, pirouettes, or tap pull-backs); sequences that require contradictory balances or footwork/directional changes; and movements which must be *made* to work (i.e. cheated or fudged) because they do not make sense physically. The dance material should cause the performers to reach, yet not go much beyond, their grasp. In creating the audition combinations, try out steps to see how accurately and easily they can be learned. You may have made up steps that you think are terrific, only to discover that the routine is not worth taking beyond this stage. Stick to steps which make sense when put together, so that each step flows logically into the next.

While the auditioning routine should be representative of what is required by the show, the show may feature more than one dance style, in which case the choreographer should offer other sample combinations. Sometimes one style will be naturally easier for an individual to copy than another style. Sometimes there will be a male-female split in the demands of the material, as in *Oklahoma!*, where the men do tap while the women do not, or as in *Cabaret*, where that situation is reversed. Taking *Oklahoma!* as an example, the men should be able to do big jumps and leaps, and at least a simplified tap or rhythmic routine for the "Kansas City" number. The girls should be able to do quicker, lighter jumps and some balletic steps for "Many a New Day" and the "Dream Ballet," as well as a stylized can-can for the number with Jud's postcard girls.

West Side Story calls for divisions in material so that the Jets dance in one style and the Sharks in another. The Jets have "Cool" to contend with as their own, the Sharks have "America," and all the performers have the dances at the gym and the "Somewhere" ballet. The men, of course, also carry the "Prologue," as well as the physical slides, lifts, leaps, tumbles, and mimes constituting their fights. *Bells Are Ringing* has a more simplistic dance load, on the other hand, requiring only a light waltz step for "Hello, Hello There" or a cha-cha by some for "Mu-Cha-Cha."

ORGANIZING THE AUDITIONS

One of the choreographer's aims in organizing auditions is to waste as little of people's time as possible, calling candidates only when they will be needed and used. Sometimes bottlenecks, obstacles, and unforeseen developments do arise, which can be unproductive and frustrating for everyone involved. The idea is to minimize these occasions by being fully prepared and doing your homework first.

When the auditions are first being scheduled, separate times should be set to see the chorus men and women. How much time should one allow for each group? The answer will depend on how many candidates there are to be seen, the amount of material to be covered, how quickly the candidates learn the material, and how long it takes the choreographer to classify their abilities.

Can the choreographer project how many will show up? Sometimes the answer is yes, as in the case of the annual school or community musical, where the turnout can be estimated from previous years. A show with a particular appeal may bring a surprise flood of aspiring candidates. The more the better, because the larger gathering will offer the greatest pool of talents, abilities, and appearances from which to choose. However, the more people seen, the longer and more complex the audition process becomes.

A usual arrangement is to have "open auditions" which anyone may attend. Once everyone has been seen and graded, those considered most desirable for the project and therefore subject to further scrutiny are invited to be seen again at a "callbacks," the audition equivalent of "semifinals" in sports competitions. Callbacks can usually be handled in one long session. The men and women are still in segregated groups, all attending the same meeting but competing only against members of their respective sexes. The "final callbacks" bring the men and women together for the first time, giving the production staff the opportunity to observe their heights, appearances, abilities, and personality chemistries.

Sometimes callbacks and final callbacks are combined into one extended session. The members of the production staff make first, second, and third choices, in case those wanted are not available for some reason. A long-running show looks for more than a cast when it holds its auditions: replacements will be needed as time goes on and cast members leave for other projects. Auditions for a long-running show, then, call for considering and classifying many more performers than will auditions for a limited-run show.

AUDITION PROCEDURES

Upon arrival, the applicants should sign a vertically numbered sign-in sheet which has been prominently posted. This sheet will set the initial sequence for seeing and later grouping the candidates. After signing in, each candidate is given a numbered index card which matches the number by which his signature is listed on the sign-in sheet. The index cards are useful for many reasons.

In amateur productions, pictures and resumés, both of which are considered essential in professional theater, are usually absent. The index card serves the purpose of the resumé by supplying information as to where and when the applicant can be reached, as well as by indicating previous training and experience. Even in professional circles, where resumés are standard, cards are often used to keep matters straight. They can be transported, rearranged, and tossed away, and are handy for making critiques and identifying grouping patterns.

A model of how the card is to be filled out should be posted beside the sign-in sheet. As shown below, the front of the index card should include spaces for the name, telephone numbers (home, business, answering service), address, age, occupation, organizational affiliations (you never know when you will need a favor or a prop from this source!), and any obligations which may conflict with the rehearsal/performance schedule. On the back of the card, the applicant should list previous training, performance experience, and any special skills.

By using blue cards for males and pink cards for females, or any other easily recognizable color-code system, you will save yourself much time when sorting the cards or searching for a particular one.

Name:	Age:
Telephone: (Home)	
(Business)	
(Answering Service)	
Address:	
Occupation:	
Affiliations:	

Figure 10–1—Sample Sign-In Index Card

How can the choreographer keep a clear record of the many contestants and their individual performances? It is essential that the choreographer remember the abilities and impressions made by each. One approach is for the choreographer to arrive with grading charts to keep track of everyone. Whether copied in advance with columns and lines, or improvised on a pad, the *grading chart* (page 131) will not only serve as a written record for later reference, but will force the mind to focus more strongly on the details of each performer.

If the choreographer is present at the initial singing auditions, he should write down what song the contestant sang, which frequently helps to spark one's memory, as do notes on clothes or hair. If it is not possible for the choreographer to attend the initial singing audition, he should certainly hear the contestants at the callbacks, just as the music director should see how the contestants move at as many of the choreography auditions as possible. Casting is always a series of group decisions.

Different circumstances will dictate which method will work better, the card system or the chart system. The chart seems most effective for singing and reading auditions, when applicants are being seen one at a time. The cards are handier for dance calls, where candidates are viewed in groups. Group evaluations call for greater organization, speed, and a method for instantly weeding out unlikely candidates. Later, when the best contenders for the show have been distilled, notes from cards can be transferred to lists, and vice versa, to maintain a complete record of the results.

The candidate choices should be reviewed as soon as possible after each session, while memory is fresh. This will reinforce any impressions and offer an opportunity to add or amend comments on the performances before a new set of applicants is presented. Another round of tryouts can, naturally, obscure recall of those who have gone before.

If the choreographer is casting for a school production, the company can include students of any age or people with irregular work hours, so he may want them to fill in availability schedules like the one on page 132, indicating when they are free to rehearse.

NAME	DESCRIPTION	SONG	BALLET #1	BALLET #2	JAZZ COMBO	NOTES
1.						
2.						
3.						
4.						
5.						
6.						
7.						
8.						
9.						
10.						
11.						
12.						

Figure 10–2—Sample Audition Grading Sheet (Filled Out to Suit Specific Show)

131

NAME _____ TELEPHONE _____

ADDRESS _____

SCHOOL ATTENDING, (IF ANY) _____

BUSINESS ADDRESS _____

TELEPHONE _____ ROLE _____

PLEASE FILL IN THE SPACES ON THE SCHEDULE BELOW, SHOWING WHEN YOU ARE BUSY.

	MON	TUES	WED	THURS	FRI	SAT	SUN
AM 8:00							
8:30							
9:00							
9:30							
10:00							
10:30							
11:00							
11:30							
PM 12:00							
12:30							
1:00							
1:30							
2:00							
2:30							
3:00							
3:30							
4:00							
4:30							
5:00							
5:30							
6:00							
6:30							
7:00							
7:30							
8:00							
8:30							
9:00							
9:30							

LIST OBLIGATIONS WHICH HAVE NOT YET BEEN SCHEDULED (EXAMPLE: UPCOMING REHEARSALS). _____

Figure 10–3—Sample Availability Schedule

If the auditions are being held in a room or studio, the choreographer's base of operations should include a table to write on, plus chairs for himself, his assistants, and any other staff members. The choreographer should be close to the piano to communicate with the accompanist, and the auditioning group should dance facing this table. However, if there is a wall of mirrors available, the dancers should perform in front of the mirrors; the reflection can work as a good educational tool.

Conditions will probably fall short of perfection; the piano may be across the room, or even in the hallway. If a choice must be made between the candidates facing the choreographer's table or the mirrors, the mirrors must take priority. The choreographer can always move from his station to sit or crouch in front of them, seeing the dancers without obstructing their view. If using the mirrors makes the candidates feel uncomfortable or cramped because of the room's shape—for example, the glass may be on the room's narrow wall—then maximum space for the performers must take priority.

If the auditions are being held on a stage, the choreographer merely observes from the house after teaching the audition routines. The use of assistants here can save a great deal of running back and forth from the stage to audience and back again.

TEACHING THE ROUTINES

Spread the candidates out in a crowd behind you, emphasizing depth rather than width. They will have a tendency to want to line up horizontally behind you in one giant line. Doing so, however, will leave them no room on either side to move, and will make it more difficult to learn or copy steps since they will have to keep looking sideways at the model. The candidates should look directly at what is in front of them, fanning out behind you. Make sure all of them can see you and have room to move. After the routine has been taught and demonstrated, rotate the crowd—the people in the rear coming forward and those in the front moving back—so that all get a chance to see clearly.

Announce the time signature or prominent rhythm used in the combination (for example, 3/4 time or cha-cha). The candidates will then know the timing framework and pattern the steps will take.

Begin with the steps and footwork, announcing which foot you are using for which step. The vocal descriptions not only explain the process, but also help those in the rear of the group who cannot see the example at the front as well. Slowly execute the step and verbally describe what you are doing, one count at a time (unless you are working with trained dancers who understand the codified names for steps in standard combinations); give the vocal counts for the timing of the steps. Add arm, hand, and head movements, coordinating them to the steps unless these actions have counts of their own with no accompanying footwork.

Describe the dramatic and stylistic dynamics of the movements. What mood is to be conveyed? Is the movement done quickly, with a pulse or accent? Does it flow, or should it be held or passed through? Repeat the movement as many times as needed, building up the speed.

Allow the dancers digestion time to absorb the material. After completing the breakdown, teaching the combination, and repeating it a few times with a group, give the dancers some time to do the combination by themselves, privately, at their own speeds. At this time, they can iron out their particular problems with the material and ask questions. Then, run the combination with them all together, again, repeating and gradually building up speed.

For dancers who have trouble remembering the sequence, an aid to reinforcing the material is "verbal visualization." The dancers should shut their eyes while you describe the steps they are learning in the performed rhythm. A verbal repeat system can also be used, where everyone recites the steps together in rhythm: if they can *say* a combination, they can usually *do* it. Both techniques can also be used at the end of a rehearsal for reinforcement and review, especially when a great amount of material has been covered or a saturation point has been reached.

If you are using an assistant while teaching the routines, be sure that his style perfectly matches the concepts you want. The assistant can help demonstrate the steps once a piece has been laid out, leaving the choreographer free to scout the crowd, making corrections and noticing talent. The assistant can also execute the routine in front of the dancers later, when they are divided into groups, and help any of them if they have difficulty remembering the combination.

CREATING GROUPS

Now that everyone has been taught the audition routines, the most efficient way to ascertain proficiency is to see the dancers perform the material in groups. Amateurs should be taught, and tested on, one routine at a time. Never have less than three or more than five or six in a group at one time: the more people you watch at once, the more spread out your focus must be, so the dancers will have to perform the routine more times for you to see them all. Four is probably the ideal group size. Once you have created a group, assign it a number.

When the individual dancer's name is announced, according to the sequence on the sign-in sheet, collect that dancer's card. Have the dancers line up as you want them and arrange the cards in the same pattern before you on the table or floor. Always double-check by calling their names once they are in position to make sure their placements correspond with that of the cards. The dancers should be staggered to move freely and offer the choreographer an unobstructed view.

Label the cards with the number of the group in which the person was seen, so that the same people remain in the same groups for different routines, if more than one routine is taught. This system will also help the choreographer to remember the individuals later, when memory conjures a vision of the group as a whole. At a later stage of the refinement process, the groups may be divided in terms of caliber or potential, but, by then, the outstanding performers should be recognizable.

Unlike singing, acting, or professional dance auditions, amateur dance auditions present the challenge of adequately testing aspirants who have varying levels of proficiency. The candidates will usually fall into one of four categories: those with some or much dance training; those untrained, but able to learn and master set combinations; those who are not quite capable of extremely strenuous or coordinated routines, yet "move well"; and those for whom movement seems an unapproachable, embarrassing hurdle.

Considering these disparities in ability, the choreographer can approach dance auditions in several ways. One method is to have separate routines, and therefore separate groups, for each level of achievement. Another solution is to divide the crowd into groups according to their abilities *after* they have all learned the general audition routine and have been primarily evaluated. Or, the choreographer may ask those who have previous training to step forward, and then give them a separate routine on the spot to check their abilities, marking their cards accordingly. Lastly, the choreographer may choose to ignore the inconsistencies in levels, knowing that the best-suited dancers will be brought together again at the callbacks.

CALLBACKS

Callbacks are different from primary "open" auditions because the choreographer has already seen these people, and chosen those who have the best potential for the show. A list should be drawn up of those who have been notified and are expected to attend. This list is useful not only for keeping track of who has shown up and who has not, but also for accommodating anyone who missed the open auditions and shows up now. Though allowing such candidates to audition now is generally frowned upon, in amateur groups, the choreographer cannot afford to turn away any prospective talent. Once attendance has been called, the choreographer adds the new arrivals to the list and has them fill out the appropriate index cards.

Once again, the choreographer needs grading charts, so re-label the chart on page 131 as "Callbacks." It may be helpful to have some new headings for the columns. Besides having a candidate sing some of the songs from the earlier audition again, the director and music director may ask him to sing material directly from the show's score, especially if the person is being considered for a specific role. They may also have him read from one or more dialogue scenes. For his part, the choreographer may re-evaluate the execution of those dance routines taught at the open audition, or give the candidates new combinations to do. Discussion with the director and music director should clarify the number of columns and types of headings necessary. As part of the creative staff, the choreographer must record his opinions concerning *all* the aspects of each performer's delivery—singing, dancing, and acting.

Here is where the choreographer gains a perspective of each individual's retention abilities and the person's motivations to practice the steps at home. Now that the candidates should be more familiar with the dance movements, the choreographer can emphasize style and further corrections. The first step, then, is to review the original audition routines with the candidates, and have them repeat the routines.

Besides watching the dance stylistics, one must find out not only *who* is most physically proficient, but in *which* areas the people excel. Amateurs sometimes perform dance material even better than dancers with some training—amateurs may grasp the style of the piece, whereas the trained dancer may look for familiar patterns and cannot break out of a certain mind-set. Amateurs and novices can surprise with abilities you would not suspect: good strength, pointed toes, turning and balancing capabilities, not to mention acting abilities. The important question is, what can these people do that the choreographer can use? Which of the candidates can do kicks, jumps, leaps, and turns? This is what the auditions, and especially the callbacks, are all about.

The candidates must also be asked about past injuries from performances, athletics, and accidents, as well as specific physical limitations or inabilities (bad back, bad knees, and so on). An injury or a physical inability does not mean that the people with such limitations cannot be used, but one should know *if* and *when* one will have to work around these limitations. You may have to choose one dance step over another to allow for someone's disability, but that is of little consequence. Let the disability challenge your inventiveness: there is always more than one dance step available to make your dramatic statement.

THE FINAL CHOICES

By the time the open auditions and callbacks are finished, you should have a pretty good idea of who can do what, having seen enough of the candidates by now to know most by name.

Now is the time to decide who best "fits the bill" in terms of technical ability, dramatic and stylistic grasp, physical type, responsibility, and pleasant attitude. Few people represent a perfect blend of attributes and liabilities. Is someone strong in one area and weak in another? Which ability is more important for the needs of the show? Does talent outweigh personality? Does a particular role call for more singing or dancing? Is the performer undeveloped in a certain area but responsive to corrections?

After seeing and grading all of the aspirants, the choreographer should list his casting preferences in order of desirability. The dance chorus, and roles which require even more dance ability, take priority. This list, along with the open-audition and callback grading sheets, will be needed at the casting session, when he consults with the other members of the production staff. More people than are needed should be on the list, since for reasons such as scheduling conflicts or a refusal by someone to play a certain part, not everyone may be available. Of course, the show's director and music director must fill their requirements as well, and may object to certain choices because of their own priorities.

Your strong preference for a particular candidate is no guarantee that the individual's casting will be unanimously approved. The music director would like a company which produces the best sound, the director would like a company of the best actors, and the choreographer will opt for the best performers in movement. Some negotiating and compromising always take place, which is another reason why the choreographer must become familiar with the way that *all* of the candidates move, speak, and sing at the auditions. The candidate that the choreographer has dismissed as a clumsy dancer may be a strong singer; on the other hand, the choreographer may want a particular dancer and have to convince the music director of the performer's vocal ability.

As for scheduling conflicts, the level of a candidate's potential contribution to the show must be considered. If someone is very anxious to partake in the production or is unusually talented, it is preferable to work around that performer's schedule to some extent, making it possible for him to appear in a segment or two, rather than lose him completely.

CASTING

Actually casting the show requires the choreographer to ask himself a number of questions. How much and what type of dance/movement is required? How much do the individual members sing and speak besides dance? What technical obstacles will the performers have to confront: costume changes, *quick* costume changes, set changes, or use of props? How many chorus people can you can have? Of that total number of bodies, how many should be singers, and how many dancers? As indicated by the script, is the cast size set, or flexible? Is the current cast's size limited by the size of the stage, the costume budget, or the amount of rehearsal time? Remember, the more people involved in the show, the more rehearsal time needed.

Dance Requirements

What dance work do the principal players have? Some principal and supporting roles have dance specialities written into their parts, such as Harry Beaton and Jeannie MacLaren from *Brigadoon*, or Will Parker from *Oklahoma!*. Some dance parts are performed by chorus members, such as the Dream Laurey and Curly in *Oklahoma!*, the Carnival Boy in *Carousel*, and all of the characters in the "Small House of Uncle Thomas" ballet from *The King and I*.

The following are examples of the kind of profile you should "work up" for the dance requirements of your production.

Oklahoma!

- Needs a good core of dancers augmented by singing chorus

- Can have an infinite number of chorus people

- Has only one principal character who is required to tap-dance as well as read lines (Will Parker)

- Has two principal dance roles: Dream Laurey and Dream Curly (three, if a Dream Jud is included)

- Dance load varies—one all-male tap number ("Kansas City"), one all-female balletic number ("Many a New Day"), one couples number ("The Farmer and the Cowman"), and a Dream Ballet which may consist of eight episodes

Brigadoon

- Needs a core of dancers augmented by a singing chorus

- Can have an infinite number of chorus people, and should, since the story is about an entire village

- Has three principal characters—Harry Beaton, Jeannie MacLaren, and Maggie Anderson—who must dance extensively, though none sing and Maggie has no lines

- Large dance load on both chorus and dancing principals—lead males have the "Sword Dance," all males join "The Chase," the females have the balletic "Come to Me, Bend to Me," plus many different couples' numbers and folk-dancing numbers

West Side Story

- All the characters must dance and sing to some degree—vocally, the Shark men have only "Quintet/'Tonight'"—except for the four "adult" roles

- Cast size is dictated by the script (since there is no chorus *per se*), but is easily adaptable

- All the dancers are principals who have to actively participate in scenes

- Emphasis on typecasting comes into play here, because the characters must fulfill certain physical requirements

A Little Night Music

- Set number of chorus people who perform only musical staging (no dancing)

- No dancing by any principals

- Cast size is set

- Heavy number load, vocally—the show has a vocal focus, so staging can be kept simple

Typecasting

To "type" people is to cast them on the basis of how they look. Naturally, appearance is fundamental to the communicative process between the performers and the audience, since all that the production staff wishes to convey can only be perceived through sight and sound. A general consensus is that actors should look as appropriate as possible for the roles they are to portray. True, much can be changed through make-up, costuming, padding, and wigs, but some disguises are easier to effect than others. Some roles hold high demands, calling for defined visual impressions. Yet the audience is willing to help along any illusion to some extent, by arriving at the show ready to accept what is presented.

It is only fair, then, to present a picture which does not strain the viewers' credibility. Size, weight, coloring, and age all contribute to the image the audience perceives. One's license to "type" in casting depends entirely upon the number of applicants one has: the larger the pool from which to choose, the more specific one's prerequisites can be.

11 REHEARSAL BASICS

The cast has been chosen, and the dance homework is ready. How does the choreographer prepare for rehearsals? By setting ground rules; making sure that the performers are wearing the proper attire; preventing dance-related injuries; investigating the rehearsal space and its facilities; and marking the dance floor with tape.

Admittedly, not everything can be worked out prior to rehearsal. Yet projecting music, grouping patterns, and floor planning on paper beforehand—foreseeing how a combination will look when performed *en masse*, or how complementary groups will function when juxtaposed—is relatively easy, just as easy as making up steps to teach one person at a time.

Some work cannot be completed when the choreographer is working alone, since certain intricate coordinations of complementary groupings or specialized material depend upon individual skills. In these cases, extra planning rehearsals should be called, if possible, for the construction of specialized routines. Using selected dancers or assistants, the choreographer should work out the more complex patterns *before* approaching the full company, building solos and special material in private rehearsals with the performers who will actually be doing the moves. This way, the choreographer can see what looks best for the performers, then tailor the dance content to everyone's advantage.

Not every move, nuance, and breath has to be established before rehearsal. Flexibility and a quickness to see what works and what does not must be maintained by the choreographer. He should be asking himself: What dance steps don't work, and why? How could they be made to work, or how can the same effect be achieved in another way? How can the steps work better?

During the initial exploratory stage, it is convenient for the choreographer to have the rehearsal music on cassette. That way, he will not have to drive the accompanist mad with endless repetition of small units of music, and he will not feel pressured by the presence of the waiting pianist. A copy of the show's score will be necessary for following along with the music and jotting down ideas about different choreographic treatments in various musical sections. The script should also be available for handy reference, should a question or the need for inspiration arise. Have a pad and pencil nearby to keep track of progress and to record developing ideas; you may also want props and costume facsimiles with which to experiment.

While privacy is fundamental to the creative tasks of the choreographer, working with an assistant during rehearsals will usually prove valuable in a number of respects. First, the assistant can serve as a model on whom the choreography can be molded and shaped, allowing the choreographer to see and evaluate his work from a distance. (This perspective is impossible to gain when the choreographer works totally alone.) Second, in working with an assistant, the choreographer gets instant feedback. When creating in a vacuum, it is often easy to get lost in one's own sense of what is being accomplished. Until the work is staged, the choreographer does not really know if his output is conveying his intentions; the active presence of others who share an interest in the quality of the work may alleviate any uncertainty. Such helpers can also sometimes help devise movements and assess the caliber of the available talent.

Finally, assistants can aid in running rehearsals. They can help teach when more than one group needs to be worked with at once; demonstrate moves while a routine is being run, so the choreographer is free to run around and correct the dancers; answer questions, tutor, or run the ensemble through routines for repetition, while the choreographer is engaged elsewhere; and act as previously-trained partners when the dances and their parts are being shown and taught.

GROUND RULES FOR REHEARSALS

Ground rules are especially important for such an endeavor, not only because a large group effort requires cooperation on the part of all involved, but also because staging and dancing are intensively physical pursuits which can become danger-ous if sloppily handled. The list of rules presented here pri-marily concerns respect for the work of others and safety measures.

Be prompt. Rehearsal time is always at a premium in terms of material to be learned and perfected, so time is not to be wasted by late arrivals. Rehearsals should begin as scheduled, as a matter of courtesy to those who are ready to work; people should arrive early enough beforehand to get changed into their rehearsal clothes and warm up their bodies.

No smoking or gum chewing. Not only is smoking un-healthy for those who do smoke, but the smoke is more annoy-ing than usual to nonsmokers when they are exerting themselves and breathing hard. As for gum chewing, with all the activity, anyone chewing gum runs a great risk of choking.

No drugs or alcohol before or during rehearsal. As coordina-tion- and concentration-destroyers, drugs and alcohol win the prize. Physically speaking, any inaccuracies brought about in speed, balance, and sure-footedness can be dangerous enough. The peril is increased when care must be taken in spacing, coordinating one's movements with others, timing, or doing lifts, situations where injurious mistakes can be made, even when one is solidly sober. Because drugs and alcohol impede learning speed and mental retention, these substances will render the user slower than usual, thereby wasting everyone's time as the user struggles to learn and remember the material.

No food. Strenuous activity soon after eating can bring on indigestion and nausea; eating in rehearsal can be distracting, and the wrappers and mess inevitably find their way around the rehearsal space. Newly dripped-on or licked hands are no fun for others to work with.

No one to leave the rehearsal area. When not participating in a dance sequence, a performer must first notify the choreographer or his assistant before leaving the room. Time should not be wasted in hunting people down.

Quiet in rehearsals. It's bad enough that the choreographer has to be heard over the music, let alone over an undercurrent of babble! Partners will always want to be discussing something with each other and, by rights, they have much to work out. They should be given time to untangle their problems when the choreographer is not actively working. The use of raised hands for questions helps to keep noise under control.

Personal hygiene. Since physical activity will cause perspiration, it is better to start clean. This topic is mentioned as a matter of not only cleanliness, but also social consideration—bad breath and bodily odors can make proximity uncomfortable, especially when working in couples. Fingernails should be kept clipped and filed to prevent harming others.

REHEARSAL ATTIRE

Be aware that because of close proximity and vigorous activity, rings, bracelets, wristwatches, neck chains, and belt buckles can all get in the way and cause injury, especially in partnering work. Care must also be taken of articles which can fly off or whip from centrifugal force—hair pins, barrettes, glasses, earrings. Long hair on both sexes should be pinned up or otherwise secured: hair can get caught during lifts or other close-couple movements, can whip people in the face, or can hit the dancer himself in the eyes.

Pants and Tops

Sweat pants, jogging pants, warm-up pants, or tights will keep the legs and body warm; retain accumulated body heat; permit a full range of movements; and allow the movements to be seen by the choreographer for correction. Shorts are not advisable, because the cooling leg muscles will invite injury—they can chill during any break, even during explanations of steps. Rule out jeans and other snug-fitting pants as well, since they restrict free movement. The men should wear athletic supporters or dance belts, and the women should wear bras.

An acceptable top would include a leotard, T-shirt, or tank top. Again, the article of clothing should help retain body heat, and be loose enough to allow full range of movement. Sweatshirts and other baggy coverings will obscure the design and execution of the movement; jackets and other open, flappable wear are out because they can strike or whip others during quick moves.

Cover-up Garment and "Sweat Rag"

A cover-up garment, such as a sweatshirt, jacket, or sweater, is necessary to prevent chilling whenever a performer is not active for periods of time. The garment is not to be worn *during* activity, but reserved for breaks and halts.

The performers should also have a towel, scarf, or other piece of cloth to use as a "sweat rag" for wiping off perspiration. A sweatband worn around the head will help keep the hair dry and prevent sweat from dripping into the eyes. The amount of moisture cascading off faces and bodies, especially in humid weather, can actually make the floor slippery in the spots where people are working. Sweat drops flying off the face and hair can hit others in the face or eyes, endangering balance and stability, and encouraging collisions and falls. Slippery hands and bodies in partner work are always hazardous.

Approximations of Costumes or Props

Rehearsal costumes and props are simplified versions of pieces to be used, approximating the type of movement that the originals will have. The simplified costumes can be incorporated into rehearsals after the steps have been taught, or can be used in the initial teaching, depending upon the degree of involvement and necessity in the dance combinations.

Shoes

The shoes to be worn and practiced in during rehearsal will be influenced by the material and traction of the floor of the rehearsal space. Resilient wood is the best floor substance, because the impact of the foot connecting with the floor will be absorbed by the wood. This absorption spares the joints of the body, so that legs will tire less easily and the chances of injury are reduced. If the surface of the floor is made of cement or tile, or there is a cement base directly under a wood covering, the impact of every move will be absorbed by the leg muscles and joints rather than be distributed by the floor. The constant shock produces straining and "shin splints," a condition in which muscles are gradually separated from the bone. Once these injuries occur, the only cure is total rest, so one cannot afford for such injuries to even begin. With this type of floor, sneakers and rubber-soled shoes can help deaden the impact some, but more frequent rests will also be required.

The issue of *traction* is an important one because the degree of slickness of the floor will dictate which movements can be done safely, and which cannot be executed at all.

When working with amateurs, the best idea is to start out by having them wear sneakers or some rubber-soled shoes until they have become accustomed to the balances and speeds of their moves; take the precaution that initially, too much traction is better than too little. Later, after the material has been basically grasped in its entirety, they can switch to their performance shoes. Not only must they get used to the minute changes brought about by the new shoes, but the shoes themselves must be properly broken in for flexibility, traction, balance, and "pointability" (the ability to display pointed feet).

Lace-up shoes which can be pulled tightly to the foot are preferable for the men. The women should utilize a shoe with a strap and buckle, to attain sure-footedness and prevent the shoes from flying off the feet when momentum or the arch of movement is high. People *can* kick shoes right off their feet! Women will often opt to rehearse in ballet slippers, but watch out for traction problems—they are not called "slippers" for nothing. An elastic strap should be attached across the arch of the foot to keep the slipper's position secure. If shoes with heels are to be worn in performance, the dancers must begin working in them as soon as possible in order to get used to the greater weight distribution and balance differences.

There are two major exceptions to all of this—tap and ballet. Tap shoes must be worn throughout rehearsals for tap numbers, so that the performer is able to hear the sounds. Tap shoes call for a different balance to be mastered; they are extremely slippery, and also have to be broken in. If ballet slippers are being used in the performance, they should be used in rehearsals as well, because the foot can only execute those steps in such shoes. The line of the foot must be seen to ensure proper corrections. Ballet slippers definitely present unique balance problems because there is a smaller base on which to balance, thus limiting the normal supportive spread of the toes.

PREVENTING INJURIES

Dance-related injuries simply cannot be afforded; the tight rehearsal schedule does not allow for a "time out" period. Preventing injuries during rehearsals—by monitoring the performers' body temperature and "workability" before and after the physical output—is of prime importance.

Make sure that people warm up before starting to rehearse. The muscles must not only be stimulated to promote circulation, but also be made pliable enough to withstand the stretches, strains, and shocks brought about by the movements. Muscle fiber is much like modeling clay: it will break easily when pulled before kneading, but attains shapability through its gradual working.

Weather and climate conditions both inside and outside the rehearsal hall can set the stage for injury and illness. Cold or even cool weather will call for slower and more extensive warm-ups. Breaks for whatever reason, including explanation time, must be minimized because the body will cool quickly after exertion, causing the muscles to stiffen while the dancer stands and listens.

Warm-up garments can help the muscles temporarily retain flexibility, depending upon the severity of the chill in the air. Warm and humid weather requires less warm-up and poses little threat of premature cooling. Air that is cool *and* humid, however, presents the greatest danger. In this situation, the body generates great heat and sweat because of the humidity, but then cools off rapidly when movement stops, so that the moisture on the skin gets chilled.

Performers should allow themselves a cooling- and drying-off period before they leave the building and are still warm from their exertions, especially in damp or cold weather. They should wear scarves, jackets, and hats when leaving rehearsals, and keep their collars closed.

Rehearsals should be structured to gradually lead up to the more strenuous material, rather than to require dancing full-out from the very beginning of the session. In this way, the bodies can warm up as the pace of the rehearsal accelerates. One approach is to teach new material first, then build up from there, as the performers become more familiar with the steps. Reviewing previously-learned routines requires a much higher level of performance energy and ability, and so should be saved for the end of the rehearsal, when dancers are thoroughly primed. "Marking" (going through the motions with understated energy) should be done at the onset of a rehearsal, so that everyone can get into higher gear for greater effort.

Muscles are basically only capable of contraction and relaxation, and it is during relaxation that they can be stretched. Major injuries include strains from over-contraction, tears from over-stretching, and strains from lifting. Such injuries can occur for a variety of reasons—balance problems, a false momentum, unpreparedness, or incapability of supporting extra weight.

Muscle injury is not to be confused with the temporary soreness or stiffness which results from unusual muscular effort. Unlike this type of discomfort, which can be worked through in rehearsals, injuries are incapacitating, causing enough pain to prohibit movement of the body part. While working with the affected muscles will help alleviate temporary soreness, doing so will increase the severity of a true injury. This is how minor injuries, if not caught in time, can turn into major injuries.

The amount of rest or exercise an injury requires will depend upon the specific damage; its cause, extent, and treatment; and the body's own ability to heal. Medical help should be sought if intense spasm or pain demands urgent relief, or if the injury does not seem to mend itself.

THE REHEARSAL SPACE

The choreographer will often have the option of holding rehearsals either on the performance stage or in a large, empty room. There are advantages and disadvantages to both methods.

When working on the stage, the actors get used to moving around in their actual performing area, thereby minimizing later adjustment. The size and placement of the steps, the spacing of the dancers, the traction of the floor, and the location of visual targets to use as reference points for spacing and spotting turns, can all be established as the steps are being learned. The choreographer is also able to sit in the house seats and watch the work from the audience's point of view. The performance stage, however, lacks mirrors (an almost mandatory teaching aid) and privacy. While the rehearsal hall has mirrors that are often readily usable, and is more private, all aspects of the accomplished work has to be altered to some degree to suit the circumstances of the stage.

Whichever type of space is used, it must have good lighting—nothing is quite as uninspiring as a dimly-lit hall. Poor lighting causes people to tire earlier, shorten their attention spans, and become lethargic; bright lights seem to keep people alert and maintain higher spirits. The need for a circulating air supply is clear to anyone who has ever been stuck in a sealed room with no windows or ventilation and tried to work with "dead air" which is neither circulated nor replenished. Fresh air is especially vital when one considers the body's need for extra oxygen during spans of activity and mental concentration.

Mirrors

The value of mirrors to rehearsal cannot be overstated. In terms of efficiency, one rehearsal with mirrors is equivalent to four rehearsals without mirrors. The dancers, being able to see their own images next to that of the choreographer, can actually compare themselves to him visually, step for step, pose for pose. Corrections make more sense because the performers can *see* what is being adjusted. The choreographer, in turn, can see what the dancers are doing in terms of his reflected example and can correct while looking in the mirror as he works. Mirrors also help ensemble and formation work become more uniform because the performers can see the entire picture with their own eyes, enabling them to judge their contribution to the overall image.

Without mirrors, the choreographer must remain in the front of the group with his back to the dancers so they can imitate his left and right movements as they all face an imaginary audience. The performers, being unable to view themselves, cannot correct their own mistakes, since they cannot see their complete image and can only *feel* their movements.

When working onstage or in a mirrorless hall, one or two rehearsals should be held at a local dance school or other facility with mirrored walls to give the performers the opportunity to see what they are doing. The difference it makes to the dancers' ability to self-correct and the improvement of the quality of the numbers is always worth the trouble of locating a mirrored facility.

However, there is one way to simulate mirrors, when performers are working at night in a room with large windows. With bright lights on the inside of the room and darkness outside, the window glass will reflect the performers' images like a dark mirror. Make use of this trick if no mirrors are available.

The Rehearsal Floor and Traction

The surface of the floor is just as important as its composition. Whether smooth or rough, the texture should be consistent: if some areas are more abrasive than others because of residue from liquids spilled in the past, the floor must be cleaned and, if necessary, sanded down. If the floor is gouged, the choreographer should try to have the cracks and holes filled in, not only for greater dancing ease, but as a safety precaution, to prevent the possibility of tripping. And if the floor's general condition is bad enough, the choreographer may opt to have the entire floor covered, with either a Marley floor (a rubber/plastic dance floor used by professional companies), sheets of plywood, or even rolled-out linoleum. The final alternative, if all else is deemed unworkable, is to structure the choreography itself around the bad or worst sections of flooring.

Traction problems were mentioned earlier in relation to attire and shoes, and these problems usually occur on surfaces that are too slippery rather than too rough. Waxed floors resist almost any treatment, save for rubberizing the shoes: most of the solutions listed below will only worsen a slippery-floor problem if the floor is waxed. For the unwaxed surface, however, the solutions are numerous.

Crystalline Rosin

Crystalline rosin is used by professional dance companies and schools as the most common and effective producer of traction short of using Marley flooring. The substance is purchased by the pound in brittle, amber pieces and chunks of various sizes, which break down into a sticky, granular powder when crushed. The powder, which adheres to the surfaces with which it makes contact, is usually kept in "rosin boxes" (shallow, square, wooden pans with a slight surrounding lip). The dancers step into the boxes, onto the rocks or granules, and rub their feet around. One box is adequate for rehearsals; two boxes are usually needed for a performance, one at the entrances on each side of the stage. The boxes keep the rosin from being wasted and spread all over the backstage area.

After some use, the rosin does have to be reapplied, depending upon the slipperiness of the floor. The constant use of rosin can cause an accumulation on the bottoms of the shoes, which in time will harden, causing slickness itself. The application of more rosin only worsens the situation. The solution is simply to scrape off the old, compressed coating with a file, knife, or any sharp instrument. Then the sole or heel should be roughed up so that the new rosin can stick to a fresh surface.

Crystalline rosin is not to be confused with *powdered rosin*, which can be bought in paint stores and is used to help bind pigment. Powdered rosin will not secure the desired traction, and its use can raise choking clouds of dust.

Cola and Cleanser

Cola, no matter what brand, will dry to a tacky residue when spilled. Sprinkled about a stage, cola can offer the desired change in traction, though certainly not all over a gymnasium floor. Application of the drink to the shoe bottoms will also help. The stipulation is that the liquid must be dried and tested. Any wet liquid will only heighten the danger by increasing the slipperiness of the floor. Besides the waiting required for drying and testing, the other disadvantage to using spilled cola is the messy cleanup.

An alternative substance to sprinkle around the floor is a powdered cleanser like Comet or Ajax. If the powder is not moistened, it can raise clouds of dust which are noxious to inhale; but if it gets too wet, the powder will turn into a white or blue mud. In cases of extreme need, the combination of cleanser on the stage and dried cola on the shoes may create the desired traction.

Treating the Shoes

Another method of creating traction is a thin coating of rubber which can be applied to the soles and heels of the shoes by any cobbler. This coating is essential for tap shoes and is generally recommended for jazz and character shoes, which appear onstage as normal street shoes. For tap shoes, the metal tap at the front of the sole and over the entire heel will offer *no* surface resistance at all, rendering the shoes almost uncontrollably slippery before the taps are worn down to the proper degree. However, when the rubber itself is new, it can provide too much traction, making turns, slides, and similar moves impossible until the rubber is broken in with use.

Leather and rubber will become worn smooth through excessive use and wear, such as extended rehearsal periods or a long performance run. Scoring the bottoms with a knife, making a series of diagonal and perpendicular scratches, will restore the shoes' original hold, as will chewing up the surface with a wood file.

Strips of masking tape on the bottom surfaces of the shoes can also add resistance. The tape only needs to be used at the points of primary floor contact—the ball of the foot and the heel. However, the assistance is only temporary, since the tape has to be constantly replaced. Tape is very efficient for covering taps that need to be silenced during scenes where they are not required to be heard or when people are walking in them backstage.

While wetting the bottoms of the shoes is the cheapest, quickest, and easiest method of achieving instant traction, it should *never* be tried on a waxed floor, where moisture will only intensify the problem. The effect does not last long, and is harmful to the shoes. A helpful hint here is to step on soaked paper towels to cut down on the amount of water applied to the shoe and limit the "wet area" backstage.

Marking the Floor

Since familiarity with onstage obstructions, levels, passage-ways, exits, entrances, and dance areas is crucial to the per-formers' movements, the designations for these future physical realities must be accurately indicated in the re-hearsal space.

The perimeter of the stage should first be measured and marked on the rehearsal floor with tape, with representations of the wing openings included on both sides. A center line running from downstage center to upstage center is next ap-plied, from which the placement markings will radiate. These markings are made at two-foot intervals along the edge of the stage, beginning at the center line and working outwards to-wards the right and left. They should be labeled symmetri-cally on both sides of the center line, from the center to the wings. Label the markings for visual clarity and verbal refer-ence as 2, 4, 6, 8, and so on, according to their distance from the center line (see diagram on page 155). The median points are understood to be 1, 3, 5, 7, and so on. All the numbers should face upstage in order to be read by the actors.

There are many variations of this set-up. For example, the numbers can be labeled sequentially as 1, 2, 3, 4, and so on. The actual measurements may vary from grid to grid, but should remain consistent within one system. The essential feature of this procedure is the exact reproduction of the scheme from rehearsal floor to the stage, guaranteeing a measured constant for placements.

AUDIENCE

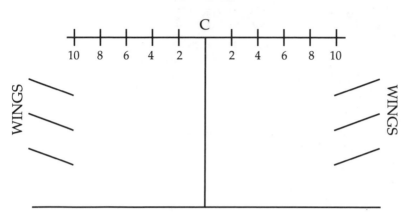

Next, tape in the different levels of platforms and stairs, with "escape" stairs (offstage exits) indicated as well. After that, tape in the set pieces. If the production requires many set changes, which most musicals do, pieces may be represented by lined-up chair backs in a row or some other easily constructable, temporary spatial divider. Stage props should be indicated as well. The pieces should be approximated by sturdy three-dimensional objects such as tables, chairs, or other crude facsimiles.

All of these markings are used by the director, choreographer, and actors as visual guides to establish placements and spacing on stage. Eventually, when the show is moved onto the stage, a replica of this system will be applied to the stage floor. Endless time will be saved in transferring musical numbers from the rehearsal space to the stage, since the placement of people is already worked out, merely requiring readjustment for the changes in visual perspective and sight lines (angles of view from the audience). This floor-marking procedure is used by many professional companies, especially when touring, so that no matter how the size of the stage varies, performer placement remains consistent.

12 RUNNING THE REHEARSALS

Dance rehearsals consist of several elements: teaching the routines, structuring the sessions, refining the dance numbers with review rehearsals, and notating the steps so that the dancers can practice them at home. In running the rehearsals, the choreographer must keep in mind that each performer has certain mental and physical limitations that will determine how quickly, and how thoroughly, he can absorb the material.

TEACHING THE ROUTINES

An effective choreographer must be a skilled, communicative teacher. What good are all the creative and dazzling dance combinations if the choreographer cannot get the performers to do the steps accurately or effectively? The teaching process in rehearsal consists of dividing the ensemble into appropriate groups for structuring and rehearsing the number; demonstrating the first steps in terms of foot patterns; naming each step pattern, adding its count and rhythm; matching the steps to a particular count system; adding arm, hand, and head movements along with body angles; creating dynamics—style, energy level, pulse, and phrasing; and providing dramatic elements and intent, relating the steps to the music to convey a specific dramatic meaning. Teaching the steps calls for breaking them down into the simplest components possible, as the choreographer explains how to do the step, which foot is doing what, where the momentum, balance, and weight distribution belong, and other pertinent information.

The actual "dancing" does not begin until the steps are executed to the music with the desired intent. The choreographer must help the dancer become "count-conscious" and wean him from the necessity to count aloud, so that he learns to associate the steps with the music while counting to himself. Ultimately, all counting must be so ingrained and "second nature" that unexpected intrusions will not interrupt the dancer's continuous movement.

Do *not*, under any circumstances, show a combination in its entirety before it is broken down and taught. A premature exhibition can cause more harm than good, creating preconceptions like "I could never do that" or "I could never look that good." The potential dancers will naturally assume a defeatist attitude which the choreographer may have to spend the rest of the rehearsal period trying to reverse.

Even when teaching, do not show a complete, polished performance of the material until the dancers have put the steps together a few times and are beginning to master the sequences themselves. While mistakes can be corrected, refinements cannot be made until the performer is ready for the next level. The amateur will try to duplicate his *impression* of the steps if he does not understand the actual mechanics. A performer cannot control the quality of a finished product unless he understands the basic parts of the movement.

Never hesitate to correct, explain, or repeat any step or section. Remember, the choreographer is the only one who knows what the work should look like and what any allowable variations might be. The performers, with or without mirrors, cannot see themselves in terms of the idealized material; they are grappling with new challenges to their physical coordination and mental concentration, as well as juggling counts and theatrical elements. At times, you may have to physically force someone's limb into position to let the performer get the feeling of the placement, or to make him see how the position should look.

Be sure to move slowly until the sequences are mastered —after all, if the dancers cannot do the material slowly, they certainly will not be able to execute it at performance tempo with any degree of control. Work the pace up gradually, and avoid suddenly shifting from a slow teaching tempo to performance speed.

If time allows, elementary movement classes should be given at the beginning of rehearsals, not only to warm up the fledgling dancers for the rigors of the session, but also to advance their physical and mental educations about their bodies. The proper exercises will expand flexibility and strength and, at the same time, encourage sensitization and control of individual body parts. Techniques and sequences based on "isolation" exercises will prove very helpful. If time does not permit group participation, explain some exercises which people can use to warm up their bodies on their own, including any special warm-up movements suitable for the choreography.

THE REHEARSAL SCHEDULE

There are basically three levels of choreographic rehearsal: blocking, running, and polishing. In blocking rehearsals, you explain the steps in terms of counts, matching the steps to the music; create and assign grouping and travel patterns; and establish the physical mechanics of the number. In running rehearsals, you repeat the dance numbers to smooth out problems and make basic corrections; pursue the dramatic foundation of the number; and get the dancers accustomed to performing the piece as a whole. In polishing rehearsals, you provide detailed dance corrections and refine nuances in movement.

The length and number of rehearsals necessary becomes easier to calculate the longer you work with a given group. With each rehearsal, the choreographer becomes more familiar with the dancers' assets and liabilities, and the dancers become more accustomed to working with the choreographer. The result is that the performers' abilities to pick up the dance work accelerates as time goes on. Amateurs who have never danced previously, and who at first can take weeks to learn a single number, gain the ability to master dance steps within one or two sessions in later rehearsals. The choreographer should also build into the schedule allowances for catch-up rehearsals, which are often required due to a variety of causes.

Where to Start

Begin with the most technically difficult or long numbers, since these will require the most amount of rehearsal. However, my experience tells me that the earliest material learned in an amateur situation is usually that which will not "clean up" as well as dance numbers covered later on. The dance combinations learned during the first few sessions are a problem, because both the choreographer and the performers are acclimating to each other. Initial learning mistakes can easily occur during this exploratory period, and once steps are programmed, they become almost impossible to change.

It is a safe idea to commence the first one or two rehearsals with a number consisting of more simplistic material which will be easier to clean up. The simplistic rehearsal will allow the ensemble to get used to the choreographer's way of working, and vice versa. This introductory stage of rehearsals is also the period during which the choreographer gets to observe the individual performers, keeping aware of the more difficult upcoming pieces to be assigned.

Pacing

It is not a good practice to concentrate a lengthy rehearsal period on one extended dance number. On the other hand, it is not a practical scheme to work on more than one number at a time. As each number is completed, it will go "into storage" so the choreographer can move on to further material. Without frequent review, these finished dances will be forgotten, or, at best, inaccurately remembered.

By building a number in stages, adding new material to that accomplished in previous sessions, the troupe will constantly review and clean up the steps already learned, even as they are run in conjunction with the newly apportioned segment-of-the-day. There is, however, a danger to this "build-a-number" method: the chance that opening night will arrive with whole numbers untouched or hurriedly thrown together. I once heard of a choreographer for an amateur dance show who used two-thirds of the rehearsal period working on nothing except the opening number. The show's premiere was looming, and nothing else had even been started!

The rehearsal schedule should be structured so that three or four numbers are begun, developed, and completed at parallel times. This teaching method will allow time to be spent on each number, as the briefer rehearsal periods for each number continually reinforce previously-covered material. When numbers are completed, new numbers are begun, still allowing for review time of the completed pieces. These reviews can often easily be scheduled into the same slots as the rehearsals for new numbers, when the choreographer is using the same people in both. For example, "Bushel and a Peck" (*Guys and Dolls*) can be run at the end of a rehearsal for "Take Back Your Mink" because they involve the same female performers. In this way, the show grows as a whole and, properly paced, will retain its energy until it peaks on opening night.

There is also the matter of digestion and saturation. With shorter rehearsals covering smaller doses of input, the performers get to better absorb whatever new material is taught, integrating it with the previous work. New people have low saturation points, becoming quickly boggled by too much to remember and getting lost in the steps. Initially, the performers should only be given as much as they can do well. However, the performers' capacity to learn will expand as their mental and physical faculties develop through use.

Sometimes a show with an extended rehearsal period will peak early, reaching its pinnacle of execution and excitement in rehearsals before it has been performed for its audience. The numbers will thus seem stale by the opening night. Professional dancers learn to prolong the peak so that the opening-night show will be at its best, whereas amateurs cannot sustain the sparkle of fresh achievement. Of course, there can be the opposite problem of the poorly-arranged schedule or a too-short rehearsal period, when the show is performed unprepared with no peak possible for even professional dancers. Therefore, the rehearsal period must be paced so that the dance material is taught properly and polished.

There are two broad approaches to distributing the dance material. The first is teaching a whole number at once, correcting and polishing later on. The other method is working on one section at a time, making corrections and moving on to the next part when a segment is mastered. The happy medium is teaching the routines in progressive sections, but with broad corrections, refining the quality later—assuming, of course, that the performers are practicing on their own time between company rehearsals.

The "whole number" approach has one fundamental drawback: if an entire number is thrown at the performers at once, explanation time must be kept to a minimum. The result of the choreographer's plowing through the dance material so quickly is that there is little chance that the performers will truly understand what the individual steps are supposed to be. Later corrections can only remedy a fraction of the damage done, because once the step is practiced incorrectly, it is almost impossible to unlearn it. Another problem is that once the performers learn all the material that they have been given, they often let the energy fade. Novice performers may even start passing judgments of their own on which sections need more polish, and which ones they can let slide by.

The one advantage of the "whole number" method is the guarantee that the material will all be covered in the allotted time. The dance material may not be performed cleanly or even enthusiastically, but it will have been taught in its entirety. Of course, this system works best with professionals— but then, that is what all their training was for.

Conserving Physical Energy

An exhausted company does no one any good. If the same people are being used throughout the different time slots and the dance material so allows, try to split the performers' workload so they will rehearse one "high-activity" dance and one more easily-staged dance number in a given session. Conversely, if the choreographer must rehearse two energetic dance numbers back to back, an effort should be made to cover material with two different groups of performers at different times, instead of making everyone dance strenuously for the entire period.

You must remember, and remind your performers, that rehearsals are very depleting because the same steps are being done over and over in endless repetition at high energy levels as the dancers strive toward perfection. In performance, or even run-throughs of the total production, the dance numbers are executed only once each, seeming short in comparison with the rehearsals, and requiring only one burst of energy. At the same time, however, there is only the one opportunity to get the steps right. No second chances exist in a live setting, and for that one performance, the number must be the best that it can be.

Parts of a Single Dance Number

If you are rehearsing parts which are specialties of a single dance number (duos, trios, split ensemble), there are two basic choices in schedule structuring. However, these two choices will depend upon how pressed the choreographer is for time, and how well he knows the steps he wants to teach before entering rehearsal.

In the first schedule choice, the dancers are called at different designated times according to the individual sections that they will be performing. The dancers arrive at one-hour or half-hour slots in order to be tutored in their material. The primary advantage of this method is that no one has to waste time waiting around while a special group receives the attention. Also, the choreographer will have more time to compose, alter, or improve specific routines, with less pressure from an impatient crowd of dancers. Although none of the sections may necessarily be completed in each single rehearsal, at least everyone will have been given material to work on, and will have learned it from the beginning with individual correction. More of these types of rehearsals can be scheduled, if necessary.

The alternative system for scheduling can *only* be used effectively if the choreographer is prepared to the last detail and quick in adaptability; this option is also helpful if he is running out of rehearsal time. All the dancers for a given number are called in at the same time, divided into groups, and spaced apart according to the different segments they are to perform, the idea being that the dancers are distant from each other, but all easily accessible to the choreographer. He travels to each group to teach eight, sixteen, or twenty-four counts of a combination for the dancers to work on at a time, while the choreographer goes on to the next group to teach them *their* steps.

By the time every group has been given a portion of the routine to practice, it is time for the choreographer to return to the first group in the cycle in order to observe the dancers' progress, offer corrections, and teach them the next sets of counts to add on to what they already know. This way, everyone gets to practice his combinations while the choreographer attends to another group and adds on consecutive material until the segments are complete. With this system, virtually an entire number can be completed in a relatively short period of time.

There are, however, several important considerations here. This type of rehearsal is most effective when the choreographer recreates choreography he is familiar with through previous use, because he will not have the time to stop and think. Hesitating to experiment with an untried combination would ruin the pacing that this system affords and make almost everyone wait around. Those dancers doled out limited amounts of combinations would quickly become bored. In addition, the steps must be relatively easy to teach and learn, or any flawed combinations that the choreographer sees later on will be impossible to correct. Consequently, this type of schedule is easier to employ once the performers have gotten used to the style of the material and the choreographer's method of teaching. It is also useful for the musical staging of large groups, rather than for a dance which may call for more intricate movements.

REVIEW REHEARSALS

Frequently, as opening night draws near, certain tightening, reviewing, or taking apart and reassembling of specific combinations will be necessary. Because steps melt down over time, and people may practice bad habits at home, *review rehearsals*, sessions specifically designed for running and improving completed dance pieces, should be scheduled. Such rehearsals prove invaluable in restoring the initial energy, focus, and style of numbers that have been completed earlier in the schedule, and can give the numbers a uniform energy level and caliber of execution. Review rehearsals can be run in various ways, depending upon the condition of the material being seen and the severity of the dance number's deterioration.

The *comprehensive notes* approach entails running the number through while writing lists of specific and general corrections as quickly as possible. The choreographer then reads these notes to the performers upon completion of the number, carefully explaining and illustrating the corrections. The dance number is run again to see if the corrections are applied, while other refinements are noted. Running a number three times or more with notes on each pass, the choreographer can clean up the work satisfactorily.

The *start/stop* system is used if more cleaning up is required than can be accomplished with notes. The dance number is performed until something is wrong, at which point the action is stopped and corrected. The number then proceeds or is started again from the top. The procedure is repeated until the flaws are ironed out. If the performer has repeated difficulty in applying a specific step, tutoring should be pursued at another time privately, rather than making everyone wait for the improvement.

The *total breakdown* method is used where the most work is required, whether on a section or an entire number. The material is literally taken apart, corrected, and re-taught count by count. This extreme, time-consuming measure becomes necessary when the ensemble is very sloppy and not performing uniformly at all, but should not be used when only one or two performers need adjustment, or when the basic style and execution of a step is wrong. The choreographer must remember that any original explanation or intention of a step may be forgotten or distorted by a performer over a period of time.

NOTATING STEPS FOR HOME REVIEW

Amateur productions rarely rehearse in a compressed period because the performers are often occupied with full-time jobs. Therefore, the performers will have time between meetings to practice on their own. Even if rehearsals are frequent, home review is essential for advancing through the material. The quality and success of the production depend upon this invested time.

The novice's mind and body are not trained for accurate, detailed retention of the combinations as taught. The memory may change the steps either to an easier version for the individual to remember, or to one which feels more natural for him to execute. If every ensemble member customizes the material for himself, the production will ultimately look sloppy. Again, it is almost impossible to re-program steps which have been practiced and ingrained incorrectly. Therefore, the choreographer must furnish the dancers with study aids for preventing memory loss and "customization" of the steps. Notes must be taken on what is rehearsed.

There are two methods of writing down the steps for home review: tap dance notation and listing notation.

Tap Dance Notation

Though this system was devised primarily for recording tap dances, it can be used for any routine because of the way it breaks steps down into words. The notation utilizes a vertical, three-line system which is read horizontally.

1. *Name of the step.* The name of the step is spelled out on the middle line, broken down into syllables corresponding to the number of sounds it creates. These sounds will signify the beats, or fractions thereof, of the count system. For example, in tap, the "flap" makes two sounds and takes more than one count to do. Because it will take counts of, say, "and-one" to perform, the word itself would be divided into two parts—"fl—ap."

2. *The foot.* The initial of the foot performing the step is
written on the line above its name: R

                  fl—ap

3. *The timing.* The timing of the step is recorded directly
beneath: R

         fl—ap

         +   1

This system can be applied to any step as long as its label can
be read in the rhythm of its execution. The same system can
easily be used for combinations in ballet, because all the steps
are clearly identified.

R	L	R	L	R	L	L	R	R
glis—sade		assem—ble		sis—sone		sis—sone		passe
+	1	+	2	+	3	+	4	5

L (front)	(on) L	R (front)
fourth (position)	pirouette	fifth (position)
6	7	8

Jazz movements can also be translated as long as the steps can
be described in rhythmic terms.

L (cross)	(on) L	R	L	R
step	slide (R foot at L knee)	step	step	leap
1	+	2	3	4

L (cross)	L	R (cross)	L
step	kick (to side)	step	step (to kneeling)
5	6	7	8

The steps can be notated with as much or as little detail as
desired, to help the student remember the work. The advantage of this system is that it faithfully reproduces a breakdown
of the steps and rhythms in the individual combinations.

Listing Notation

This method consists of making vertical columns to match
the number of counts in a dance phrase. In the case of the

common eight-count phrase, the numbers one to eight would be listed, leaving a line or two for each number. Each set of numbers would be headed by a letter or Roman numeral to signify the sequence in which the eight-count phrases should be read.

A (or I)	B (or II)	C (or III)
1	1	1
2	2	2
3	3	3
4	4	4
5	5	5
6	6	6
7	7	7
8	8	8

Now the steps would be listed next to their appropriate counts in the phrase, including the "and" counts where necessary, and an indication of which foot is performing the action.

A (or I)
1. kick R
2. leg down
3. kick L
4. leg down
5. step R
+ step L
6. step R
7. kick L
8. leg down

This system emphasizes the *sequence* of steps rather than the intricacies of the steps themselves, and should be used when the performers need to be reminded of the order of the steps in a routine of extended length.

While both notational systems may be used in the course of a production, only one or the other system should be employed for a specific musical number to save confusion. The chosen system will depend upon the area of difficulty for the performers—step execution or sequence.

Once the choreographer has taught a notation method to the dancers and starts to run through a number, they should make their own charts of the steps. This handwritten process will serve as a good mental review, as the dancers are forced to examine and analyze the parts of the steps and combinations in order to write them down correctly. Once these sheets are completed, people doing the same dance should exchange papers and follow each other's instructions to try and recreate the dance.

13 BEFORE, DURING, AND AFTER THE PERFORMANCE

Having moved through all the stages of mental and physical development necessary to create and apply the choreographic material, we now come to the *raison d'etre* of these explorations—the performance itself.

FINAL ADJUSTMENTS

As exciting and fulfilling as the "home stretch" toward opening night may seem, there is still some fine-tuning to do. Because the rehearsal set-up can only go so far in mimicking the realities of the performance stage, all the work accomplished thus far must undergo conversion to the new environment. The dancers will have to be properly spaced apart onstage, familiar with the sets and the lighting, and conscious of how they will relate to the audience.

Spacing

Proper spacing ensures that those performers who should be seen *can* be seen, that choreographic patterns are clear, and that the audience is focused on certain performers. Placements and distances on the stage must be pinpointed, to avoid having people crash into other bodies, costumes, props, or scenery, and to assure that the choreography is making use of the areas of designed lighting.

This performance spacing is established by having each performer find visual guidelines, both on and around the stage, by which he can gauge his position. As noted in Chapter 11, the center line and two-foot markings should be taped down on the floor of the stage. "Spike marks" (labels on the floor that indicate placements of set pieces and stage props) can also be used. However, to avoid the disconcerting sight of all the dancers continually looking down at the floor to find their positions, have them choose items at eye level to serve as standards for measurement, such as exit signs, pillars, aisles, seating sections, specific rows of seats, markings on scenery, and lighting instruments. However, performers should be wary of relying on markers in the auditorium which may disappear when the house lights are turned off and the stage lights flashed on.

The objects most easily seen by the onstage company will be the downstage performers in the front. These are the people who can locate the two-foot markings on the edge of the stage most readily. If you place the best performers downstage, not only are they out front for the audience to see better, but they can serve as models for the chorus members in executing the dance movements and properly spacing themselves apart on the stage.

Before opening night, there should be a "cue-to-cue" spacing rehearsal. With the performers onstage, the choreographer, seated in the audience, runs through the dance routines from one formation to the next, setting suitable positions for all members at all times. He gives the performers a new set of conditions to consider after the execution of each new step, that is, finding which mark they are supposed to be on at what time. By this point, absolute mastery of the choreography is a must!

Set pieces should also be included in the spacing rehearsal. If the set pieces were accounted for during rehearsals, adjustments will be minimal, but some adaptation is always required.

Once the dancers have starting positions, they should go through the musical number in its entirety, first as a "stop-and-go," fixing problems where they occur, and then nonstop, with review of notes afterwards. This process gives the performers a chance to acclimate themselves to moving around the stage and lets the choreographer view the effectiveness of the work from different areas of the house.

Spacing arrangements are always shifting because no one will be in exactly the same spot as he was during rehearsals. Adjustments must be made to ensure that everyone is seen: if a performer is out of place and is blocking someone else from the audience's view, the person being hidden should move so that he is exposed.

Technical Details

By the time the performers move onto the stage, they should have handled and experimented with costumes, props, and other technical elements on their own time, as well as in company rehearsals. By show time, the performer must feel completely comfortable with any object he will be handling during a musical number.

The actors should familiarize themselves with the sets for function, spacing, construction, and general performance use. Knowledge of function is essential—knowing how doors, windows, and other practical mechanisms work, in which direction they open or close, and whether they jam, stick, or require any assistance in use. The sizes of these openings must be considered in terms of the numbers of people to be using them at once, including the dimensions of costume pieces and props to be conveyed through them. Can a crowd exit all at once? Do the escape stairs leading off a platform only allow one person to pass at a time, causing a bottleneck and ruining the illusion of the scene? Give the performers time to work these matters out comfortably and under supervision, to prevent panic when the pressure of opening night takes over.

One of the basic elements of any stage delivery is being seen, and being seen is dependent upon the lighting. If your production meetings have been successful, the lighting designer has understood the needs of the choreography and has attended some of the rehearsals. If the choreographer himself has stood in as a model or consultant when the lights were hung and focused, there should be few problems later, when the company is performing under lights for the first time. If the lamps cannot be easily readjusted once they have been set, and minor changes are required, move the actors into the lit areas and reassign their spacing-number markings. This alternative should be avoided when possible, however, since some performers, carrying a full mental load of new production details already, may become confused by last-minute changes in their material.

If time permits, quickly teach the dancers the difference between dancing in brightly lit, dimly lit, and dark areas. The lack of light will affect people on the edge of large groups more so than those in the center. Dancers on the periphery of lit groupings in central areas must be aware of when they can be seen. Sometimes, the lit area is less than two feet away, and the performer can subtly shift himself into it with small movements; other times, a performer will actually be moving in and out of the light, totally unaware of the disconcerting effect until he is told about it. If the dancers are to be seen in muted or partial lighting, they must be informed of the desired lighting effects so that they can help in the visual achievement.

Focus

Now that the performers are no longer rehearsing in the mirror, or watching the choreographer for corrections, where do they look when they are on stage? Coordination is necessary, because different placements of focus will convey different dramatic values. The entire onstage ensemble must agree for the message to be clear to the audience.

When facing straight out front at the audience, are the performers looking at a distinct point? Do they follow specific action offstage? Does their focus cross over the audience, such as in the "Ascot" scene in *My Fair Lady,* the "Joust" in *Camelot,* or the "Fox Hunt" in *Mame*? If presenting a number directly *to* the house, do the performers look straight out, up, or down at the audience? Some of this focus work will depend upon the layout of the theater and the location of the audience. Which sections of the audience (balconies, orchestra section, or main body) should the performers play to?

Looking at each other usually denotes conversation, as in a crowd scene where people confer. A point of action, holding the attention of all onstage, will indicate its importance to the audience by the intensity with which it is being regarded by all. All the faces and eyes aimed at one target will naturally lead the audience to the chief subject by artistic design, leaving the viewer with nothing else of interest to watch. If such a subject is offstage, the performers' focus there anticipates an entrance or revelation.

With a *front focus,* which refers to the presentation of a dance number or dance sequence directly to the audience, the performer must find distant points to use as visual references when turning ("spotting"), or when holding positions balanced on half-toe. Front focus requires the performer to be aware of the dramatic intention behind a musical number. He should communicate a mood and meaning appropriate to the number, rather than maintain a frozen, expressionless facade that masks an underlying concentration on technique.

WARMING UP

While professionals do their own warm-ups before a performance, the amateur situation calls for a group warm-up to guarantee that all will be ready to perform at peak efficiency. The company warm-up should cover all the body areas, while specific areas needing more attention should receive private emphasis afterwards, since each dancer will have his own physical strengths and weaknesses.

The warm-up should be thorough yet brief, because there are many other pre-performance considerations, such as make-up, costumes, and vocal warm-up. The warm-up must also be brief to conserve energy for the performance rigors ahead. It is not uncommon for teachers and choreographers to conduct pre-performance warm-up classes that are so strenuous that the dancers are too fatigued to deliver the material well. Nervousness alone will escape the body in violent spurts, leaving the victim feeling drained as he struggles to suppress his "flight or fight" instinct. Consequently, the performer, as opening night draws closer, may experience a schizoid period of outburst and lethargy, both caused by the mounting tension.

Nervousness will make the muscles of the body tighter than usual, ready to tense into action. Care must be taken not to rush the exercises; a soothing tone must be adopted, and at least one mental-physical relaxation exercise should be included. If properly conducted, the warm-up can help channel negative energy toward positive use, through stretching the tightened muscles, using up some of the adrenaline, and helping the performer find mental security in a familiar situation.

The warm-up should precede the application of costume and make-up; otherwise, the costumes may get sweaty and dirty and the make-up will run. The usual rehearsal attire should be required for heat retention and flexibility. Since the body will cool down afterwards, the performers must be encouraged to repeat key exercises which will warm up body parts directly used in the choreography. The most desirable state is *staying* pliable and prepared. The choreographer must encourage the dancers to minimize the length of inactivity and degree of cooling after the general warm-up is completed. During the performance itself, some cooling and stiffening will occur as the dancers first use their muscles, then wait for the next musical number. If waiting offstage, they should know how to re-warm themselves before appearing in the next sequence.

The exercises should eventually concentrate on those body areas to be heavily used in the choreography. If there are high kicks, the legs must be stretched; if there are lifts, the arms, shoulders, and backs must be limbered up; if there is to be extensive bending of the back, it must be made flexible.

Begin the warm-up with body movements that will increase overall circulation slowly, like bending the body, or quickly, like jumping jacks or light jogging. Once the blood is pumping and some body heat is being produced, isolate the different parts of the body. Warm and limber these body parts one by one: head and neck, shoulders, arms, upper back, chest, sides, lower back, and, finally, the hips. From the hips, move on to the legs, which call for treatment all their own.

The legs should be exercised with contracting movements, such as demi- and grand pliés, which will increase blood flow and coax the muscles and knees to greater pliability. When correctly executed, the pliés will contract and stretch the thigh and knee, only partially stretching the calf, so some calf-contracting movements (relevés) must be included.

Toe-pointing movements should come next, such as tendus and dégagés, calling the entire leg, foot, and hip mechanism into play, moving toward total leg involvements such as light jumping. The pliés, tendus, and dégagés should be executed in both first and second position. If time and energy permit try the exercises in third, fourth, and fifth positions as well.

Assuming that a ballet barre is unavailable, leg stretching should be done on three basic levels: sitting or lying on the floor, standing and bending to reach the body to the leg, and raising or kicking the leg up in the air. A sense of progression is the key to safeguarding against injury. The warm-up can be done in a cycle, alternating the exercises, returning to the same ones over and over, while each time reaching farther as the muscle acclimates to new length.

The session should end with a relaxation exercise that includes movement, not just a mental exercise. At the end, the performer's body should release whatever tension remains, but not by suddenly stopping movement or by immediately beginning to cool off. A slower, more gentle activity like *stacking* is ideal at this point.

In stacking, the dancer starts in a comfortable standing position with eyes closed. He tips his head to his chest and continues to curl his spine forward, slowly dropping his body with gravity, eventually bending his knees to spare strain to the lower back, and ending up as a collapsed mass, still on his feet. After a brief pause, he slowly brings himself upright again, starting at the base of the spine, straightening his knees as his body passes his waist, gradually resuming his standing position. The head raises off the chest, and the eyes finally open. The mental focus of this exercise is on the spine as it moves, vertebra by vertebra, releasing the body on the way down and pulling together on the way up—a feeling of "unstacking" and then "restacking" the bones one on top of another is the desired result.

THE PERFORMANCE

Opening night creates a panic all its own. As choreographer, you will be one of the authorities that the performers turn to for assurance, support, and advice. You should appear excited but not nervous, though you may feel very knotted-up inside. No matter how important changes may seem to you, do not make any at the last minute; the performers have enough to remember. Nerves may alter your perceptions as well, so it is safer to leave things as they are.

You should address the company with a pep talk. However, such a talk falls first to the director, who is the acknowledged leader of the show. The director's relationship with the cast members will be of a different tone than the choreographer's, as his demands have not been as physically grueling. If you deliver the pep talk before the warm-up, it will be premature, and its effect will have worn off by curtain time. But if you present the talk immediately after the warm-up, it will cause people to stand immobile and begin to cool. Give the performers that support, confidence, and energy just before the curtain rises, so that the positive charge is taken directly on to the stage.

The dancers need to be inspired. Besides telling them, "Go out there and be great," you might want to say: "*I* know you can do it. I've seen what you can do in rehearsal. *You* know you can do it. You've already done it!" In addition, you could add, "The audience *wants* to like you. Show them what you can do!" Be humorous, but also sincere—after all, you have been working with these people for some time now in all kinds of moods, so they can easily see through any pretense. Thank the dancers for the time, energy, trust, and cooperation that they have given. End the session with a group hug, cheer, or supportive gesture, sending them out, like a team coach, with an energy high. After this, gracefully disappear. Not only will it be anticlimactic for you to be seen now, but your hidden nervousness may send you seeking whatever support you can find, and it is unfair to foist your needs onto any of the performers.

During the show, stay out front, either in the audience or behind it, and take notes. Do not dash backstage after every number to see the performers or tell them anything—do not dash anywhere. The dancers are on their own, and if they have learned well from you, have faith that it will shine through.

Do not go backstage at intermission unless some general technical adjustments are called for, such as telling them, "We can't hear you." Why? Because you will be put on the spot. Everyone will want to know how you think the performance is going. Your facial expression and mannerisms, if not your words, can unduly influence the dancers. If they seem to be losing spirit and more encouragement is necessary, address the company as a whole. Limit your comments to only those aspects of their performance that can affect the upcoming act, and do not discuss any first-act mistakes. Be aware of moderating your praise or criticism. If the performers feel they are doing either too badly or too well, they will lose control of their perspective of the work. If they are told that the first act was bumpy, the dancers may try too hard in the second act; if they hear that the first act went well, they may slack off.

Once the show is over, your main concern as choreographer will be whether there is another performance to follow. If there are more to come, comments must continue in the same vein as those during rehearsal—complimenting and encouraging, but always leaving room for improvement. Answer questions and problems at a later general-notes session, and restrict your comments to the work as a whole—in other words, keep your statements "official." If, however, that performance was on closing night, you can finally tell them outright that they were great without any of the usual reservations; if they did not do well, you could make some constructive comments.

TAKING NOTES

The notes you take during performance should point out mistakes, improvements, areas needing improvements, and technical corrections. The dancers will already know when they have done well or fallen short of the mark. Therefore, the choreographer should concentrate on elements of which the performers may *not* be aware—the non-self-correcting mistakes.

Comments about the obvious mistakes should be avoided. Blatant mishaps like tripping or forgetting steps need not be mentioned, because the performer knows of the incident and will only be embarrassed if you draw further attention to it. If, however, someone has salvaged a situation on the spot through quick thinking or action, credit should be given, and the handling of the gaffe can serve as an example to the others.

There are four basic methods of taking notes during the performance: cassette dictation, dictation to an assistant, writing, and videotape.

Cassette Dictation

The primary advantage of dictation is that there is no need to look away from the stage to write and so miss some of the action. However, talking into a cassette recorder will often disturb the nearby members of the audience. If a word or phrase on the tape is unclear, there is no way to decipher it. Taped notes also prove difficult to edit or add to later, though they can be transcribed while the show is still fresh in the mind.

Dictation to an Assistant

Dictation to an assistant eliminates dealing with tape, and again, there is no need to divert one's attention from the stage to notate. The assistant can also serve as a witness to help remember those details you cannot quite recall. Unfortunately, as with the previous system, the notes must be transmitted orally, and if the comments can be heard by the assistant, they can also be heard by other spectators. In addition, the assistant will need a light to see by—another distraction for neighboring viewers, unless the light is heavily gelled. The assistant must also be present to translate the notes for you when you read them to the cast, especially if the notes are in the assistant's own system of shorthand.

Writing

Writing your own notes seems to offer the most advantages and fewest liabilities. You can write down exactly what you mean, or use abbreviations that can be filled in later. Because you are creating the notes yourself, they have more power to aid recall when reviewed. The notes will need no interpretation by another and are written in silence during the performance, which disturbs no one.

Unless you can write without looking down, however, you will miss some of the stage action while thus engaged. If you have to see the note page, you will need a light source—which can be distracting and which, even when small, can be difficult to maneuver while juggling a clipboard and pen. The solution, then, is to take the notes without looking down, an ability which improves with practice. A broad felt-tipped pen works best for guaranteed ink flow and additional clarity in the dark. Disregard lines on a page, scrawl the message, and make sure not to go over space already covered. Then review the notes as soon as possible after the show for translation and clarification.

If you are taking notes on the musical numbers only, get into the light to check them and add further refinement for yourself. Most notes will be taken in some abbreviated form for the sake of speed, so elaborate upon them and fill them out while the images are fresh in your mind, before presenting them to the performers.

Have the names of the numbers or their internal segments as headings on paper, so that you will know which corrections apply to which numbers. When preparing to scribble in the dark, pre-title the pages ahead of time, allowing at least a page for each division, and, very frequently, more than one page. It is better to allot too much paper than too little.

Videotape

A modern aid to constructive criticism can be found in the videocassette recorder. If numbers and sequences from a show are taped and viewed by the performers with the director or choreographer serving as guide, errors or areas needing improvement can be pointed out, helping the actors to see how the corrections should be applied.

The only drawback to using videotape lies in the potential for differences of opinion. Ironically, while the camera captures a performance faithfully and unequivocally, the results are so open to interpretation that they can be disputed by almost anyone. When the choreographer and director are the only members of the company who actually see the performance, their opinions will carry more weight than in a situation where the amateur can view his own delivery and judge whether he feels the corrections are worthwhile or not. Such judgments, in a way, can undercut the evaluations of the senior members of the production staff.

READING THE NOTES TO THE COMPANY

When the post-performance notes are to be given to the company, assemble the performers and make sure they have pencils and paper to list the comments they will receive. Have them sit in groups according to their casting divisions: singing men, singing women, dancing men, dancing women, principals, and so on. This segregation will save much time (directors will not have to search the crowd for each individual to be addressed) and will also allow the directors to speak to several groups at once. Once these groups have been established, they should remain part of all successive notes sessions.

As you explain how things should be done, show examples of correct and incorrect execution, but take care not to mock. It is too easy to embarrass someone by an exaggerated public imitation of his mistakes. Maintain speed, humor, and energy before the group. Now that the show has been performed, your rapport with, and mutual respect for, the cast should allow a certain amount of ease and humor. No matter how well the comments are presented, people will be anxious for them to be done with; the notes are inevitably standing in the way of more important things to do.

When is the best time to deliver the notes? If notes are given directly after a show, the performance will still be fresh in everyone's minds, as will the corrections discussed. The disadvantage to this is that although the performers have time to think about the comments, they do not get to apply what they have learned until the next evening, leaving a full day of distractions in between. If the notes session is held before a performance, not only can they apply the notes from the previous show immediately, but the references to the upcoming show will help them review the material. The problem then can be that there is not *enough* time to implement any changes; references to the previous night may also be unclear, so carefully review your notes.

The best method, then, is to divide the notes into those concerning changes that require some time for the performers to apply, and those notes that represent minor problems. The former type should be delivered individually to performers after a general presentation; the rest of the notes should be saved for a notes session just before the next show.

CONCLUSION

Creating choreography for musical theater can be a daunting, and often puzzling, endeavor. The show has a script, which includes dramatic episodes and musical numbers, and a score, which comprises all the music. There is a director, a music director, and a production staff with scenic, costume, and lighting designers. How does the choreographer put all these pieces together for the purposes of creating and staging dance?

The work can be challenging from the outset. After all, choreography is not all dance. The choreographer is called upon to devise any specialized movements not only for the musical number, but for the entire show—he may even have to stage a fight scene. The *mise-en-scène*, the music, the steps, and his imagination all form the raw material. As he builds from static poses through counted routines through combinations performed to music, he is really inventing a new language with every show, using the vocabulary of human movement and drawing upon the abilities of the cast members.

Too often, the choreographer can be afraid to try something new because of the mystique surrounding the original production. A director may treat the script and score as if they have been handed down from on high, and cannot be tampered with. There can be nothing more artistically stifling than this attitude. True, there are certain aesthetic limits to

182

what the choreographer can do. But the original production had a big budget, a Broadway stage, lavish costumes, and a professional cast; the amateur setting offers none of these. The key to good choreography is *working with what you have*— respecting the physical and mental limits of the dancers, staging the production around the available performance space, working with less-than-ideal rehearsal conditions.

We have seen how the choreographer, lacking any notations passed down from earlier productions, uses the script and the score as a framework for structuring dance sequences. The script offers descriptive clues about the style of a musical number and how it fits into the "world of the show"; the score is the choreographer's "map"—he marks off counts, blocks, themes, moments, and mood shifts in the music, adding his own accents, later matching movements to these divisions. Musical staging calls for the choreographer to play director, taking the words and music of a song—which can often work against each other—and arranging onstage movements that express a character's emotional state.

In structure, a dance piece should be like a good novel: it should have exposition, a sense of conflict, an element of surprise, and a rising motion toward a climax. The choreographer achieves these qualities by looking for a "plot line" to mark in the dance number's music, choosing the right steps to correspond to his notations. By sketching a floor plan, he can keep track of which dancers will be moving where. He assigns portions of the dance material to different groups of dancers, because having the groups do complementary step patterns, illustrates changes in the music, and draws audience attention to certain parts of the stage, creating variety and excitement.

Planning dance movements includes accounting for costumes, scenery, props, and lighting as early on as possible. For example, costumes can be too slippery to grasp, too long, or too bulky; shoes can throw the performer off-balance; and there may not be enough room backstage to accommodate all the dancers. Anticipating how these technical elements will affect onstage movement is crucial for the choreographer.

For dance auditions, the choreographer starts teaching the steps he has assembled, evaluating potential cast members on the basis of their learning ability, technical proficiency, potential, and overall attitude. He uses index cards and grading charts to keep track of the candidates, and has them try out in groups. Moving through open auditions and callbacks, he considers the show's particular dance requirements and works with the production staff to make the casting choices.

The choreographer then runs dance rehearsals, having set certain ground rules and establishing proper rehearsal attire for the performers. He shapes and teaches his material according to the mental and physical abilities of the dancers, avoiding stress-related injuries. He also does his best with whatever rehearsal facilities are available, marking the dance floor with tape so that the routines can be easily transplanted to the performance stage. Review rehearsals are scheduled, and the performers learn to notate their steps to review them at home.

As opening night approaches, there are some final adjustments to be made: checking the dancers' positions and spacing on the performance stage; making sure they are familiar with the costumes, sets, and any props they will be using; showing them how the lighting effects will work with their movements; and determining the proper focus for each number. During the performance itself, the choreographer watches from the house and takes notes, avoiding the backstage area. He delivers the notes to the dancers after the show, but reviews some of the notes with them just before the next performance, if there is one.

The choreographer has one responsibility, however, which overarches all of his work in dance and movement: motivating the dancers. Keeping the performers upbeat, enthusiastic, and driven can be as exhausting as dancing, but it must be done. Here, then, to conclude, I would like to share with you a speech that I have heard given to many an ensemble.

There are two types of show that a group can work on. There is the production where the show is put together, everyone has a good time socially on an equal basis, the audience expects little and laughs at the effort of the performers, and a big cast party follows the closing, after which all go their separate ways, vaguely remembering what was done and assuming they know something about the theater.

The other kind of show occurs where you meet new people with whom you work hard toward a common goal, learning to do things that you didn't know that you'd be able to do, caring about your contribution to something larger than yourself, and surprising an audience with abilities and a quality of production completely unexpected.

Afterwards, with this second type of show, there is the terrific satisfaction of a difficult job well done, the reward of the earned applause, the goal reached, a strong alliance with your co-workers, and a new-found sense of accomplishment. Then the cast party: a victorious celebration well earned, followed by stored memories of your own persistence and a new perception of self-worth to be drawn upon in years to come. This type of show entails hard work, but produces a different kind of fun—the gratification of working hard and achieving worthwhile knowledge and ability.

I do this second kind of show. It is not easy but it can be a lot of fun. Once things are rolling, everyone's work becomes dependent on each other's. Everyone becomes increasingly important. If it sounds like too much effort, people can drop out now. We don't want people complaining later because the production wasn't the party they expected. For a gathering of pure social fun, you can meet anywhere, anytime. But if you stay on, you'll share in an enriching experience you will carry with you for the rest of your lives.

APPENDIX:
THEATRICAL RESEARCH SOURCES

The musical theater choreographer is responsible for presenting the intent of the show's original production. While he expresses the show's dramatic meaning through steps and dance movements of his own creation, he must also draw upon sound recordings, books, magazines, and other media for guidance as well as inspiration. By setting the original production in an aesthetic, social, and historical framework, theatrical research helps the choreographer create his dance work.

Theatrical research begins with the study of the show's original production. After you read and analyze the script and score, gathering further details is necessary to provide a more complete picture. There are soundtrack recordings to listen to; print sources to read and explore; cultural factors to consider; and topical/historical events to use as sources of information about a particular production.

SOUND RECORDINGS

There are several different formats in which the musical numbers of the show are available. The **original cast recording** will give you the best idea of the show's original sound and orchestration, as well as the vocal dynamics used. Because there is rarely room on a record, tape, or compact disk for extended sequences, and dances are usually the first to go, the shortening techniques themselves can suggest ideas for any cuts that your production requires. Sometimes snatches of dance arrangements are included to help break up the vocals and give a flavor of the original number. These are valuable to the choreographer because, even in their abbreviated state, they offer full orchestration, tempo, and mood. The *Brigadoon* recording, for example, includes sections of the "Bonnie Jean" and "Come to Me, Bend to Me" dances. True, they do not mean as much in comparison with their full stage usage, but they do lend a sample of the show's feeling.

Occasionally, an entire orchestrated piece besides the overture will be recorded. The complete "March of the Siamese Children" has always been included on albums of *The King and I,* and such numbers as "The Spanish Panic" from *Once Upon a Mattress,* or "Rag Offen the Bush" from *Li'l Abner,* are heard in their entirety.

One definite advantage of albums and compact disks over cassette tapes is the production information to be gained by reading the liner notes, which frequently supply background, review quotes, a brief description of plot, and biographical information about the leads and the authors.

The **soundtrack recording of the movie** usually provides no sense whatsoever of the original work, since the vocal and orchestral arrangements have been drastically altered. The entire score may have been rewritten, along with the plot, setting, and characters. However, from such massive adjustments and the application of new material, one can get new ideas for the numbers and lyric replacements. The film soundtrack is often a treasure trove of substitute or inspirational material.

Sometimes, though rarely, material written for the movie will be interpolated into the show's stage score. "Better Than a Dream" from *Bells Are Ringing* is an example of this. After the film version of *West Side Story* was released, there were staging and musical changes in the stage score. The movie's lyrics for "America" were used onstage in some productions, the

Shark men were added to one scene which was formerly an all-girl number, the "Dream Ballet" was frequently cut, and the slots of "Cool" and "Gee, Officer Krupke" were transposed to correspond to their running order in the movie. Stage versions of *Cabaret* were suddenly including "Mein Herr" and "Money Makes the World Go Around" after the show's cinematic model.

The last group of audio recordings to be considered are those made of **revivals**. While not necessarily duplicating the vocal types found on the original cast recording, in many ways the revival recording will prove the most serviceable for research needs. Frequently, not only will the music be taken precisely from the stage score, but also, due to advanced recording techniques, the sound quality will be superior to the original cast recording, and each record side (or compact disk) can hold more music.

PRINT SOURCES

There are many sources of printed background material which provide both text and pictures about any show and its birth.

Back in the Golden Age of Musicals, primarily the mid-'40s through the mid-'50s, there were **magazines** specializing in pictorials, as well as articles, on what shows were current and of interest to the public. Look up reviews of the original production, not only in the New York newspapers (there were many more then than there are today), but also in such magazines as *Look, Life, The Saturday Evening Post, Time, Newsweek, The New Yorker,* and, later, *New York Magazine.* These reviews will offer opinions about the production's strengths and weaknesses. How was the show received in general? What was the show famous for? Has the reception changed over time? Why and how?

Back issues of old trade publications such as *Theatre Arts* (1933–80), as well as current ones like *Theatre Crafts, American Theatre,* and *Dance Magazine* can prove enormously beneficial. *Theatre Arts* includes a complete script per issue, with photographs, and features articles on the technical aspects of production. These articles highlight the procedures followed by an ongoing play and the show's director to create specific effects. *Dance Magazine* has historically focused on the Broadway, film, and television scenes, noting innovations and contributions to the field as the state of the art has continued to advance.

Souvenir playbills of the original show and its revivals (the ones bought, not those distributed *gratis*) are valuable for their photographs of the show and other pertinent information.

Books are the starting point for research in any field. The most useful are autobiographies and biographies, anthologies of collected musicals, and works about the history of particular productions. One book of particular interest to any choreographer would be *Hoofing on Broadway: A History of Show Dancing* by Richard Kislan (1987/Prentice-Hall).

The creator of the choreographic work, or a show's producer or director, has the personal information to explain the process of coaxing a concept into a reality. In this respect, the autobiographical accounts are without equal. Few write with the clarity and ardor of Agnes DeMille, whose struggles and passions for her standards, as described in *Dance to the Piper and Promenade House* (1982/Da Capo), prove both fascinating and inspiring to the aspiring dancer/choreographer. Alan Jay Lerner's autobiography, *The Street Where I Live* (1980/Norton), dispenses with his life in the first, brief chapter, then recounts backstage stories about the creation of *My Fair Lady, Camelot,* and *Gigi.*

Biographies of those figures who were continually involved in the field, such as Brian Appleyard's *Richard Rodgers* (1986/Faber & Faber), contain balanced chronologies between private and professional times. Craig Zadan's biography of Stephen Sondheim, *Sondheim and Co.* (1986/Harper & Row), takes a broad perspective of Sondheim's works through interviews with his various collaborators, defining and exploring a range of topics related to musical comedy production.

An anthology of musicals refers not to a collection of scripts bound together in a single volume, but to a text that supplies plot summary and background information covering a wide range of shows. David Ewen's *The New Complete Book of the American Musical Theatre* (1980/Holt, Rinehart, and Winston) provides pertinent facts about virtually every major American musical produced from 1866, describing nearly five hundred productions. *Broadway's Greatest Musicals* by Abe Laufe (1977/Funk & Wagnalls) scans fewer productions, limiting itself to only those that ran a minimum of five hundred performances, but more than compensates by relating extensive data about each show, its run, reception, tours, and derivation.

Books which trace the chronological paths of hit shows will point out the reasons for a given production's triumph, indicating the innovations, contributions, and precedents it set. Like similar retrospectives of the film industry, these volumes often contain interesting photographs of productions, and are frequently designed as "coffee-table books." The best of these are *Theater in America* by Mary Henderson (1988/Abrams) and *The World of Musical Comedy* by Stanley Green (4th edition, 1984/Da Capo)—which covers the composers and lyricists of various periods and their successes. *Broadway Musicals* by Martin Gottfried (1979/Abrams) and *American Musical Theatre: A Chronicle* by Gerald Bordman (1986/Oxford University Press) offer commentary on specific productions, explain their production elements, and in Gottfried's case features stunning photographs. *A Pictorial History of the American Theatre* by David Blum (1986/Crown) contains rare black-and-white photographs, as do the annual volumes of *Theatre World*.

Books on musical comedy theory and practice will generally instruct in terms of analysis, composition, and procedure; Lehman Engel's books are exceptionally valuable for his insights in the field. Books about movie musicals will not contribute much in the way of text, but the photographs in these books can provide the choreographer with inspiration for the show's time, place, style, and arrangement.

CULTURAL CONSIDERATIONS

Another important type of research is cultural. Every show, while set in a particular time and place, exists in a world of its own, and stylistically modifies the features of its setting to suit the production and the audience.

Is the show set in the '20s, the '40s, the '50s, or another time? Is it set in New York, Berlin, Paris, or Dogpatch, U.S.A.? It is very important to immerse yourself in the culture and the moods of the particular setting. Besides studying photographs, listening to the right music can help you understand the native temperament. Films from the show's time and place can also contribute greatly here. Don't we often feel we know the Victorian era, the Roaring Twenties, or the Depression because of various films?

The choreographer's concern, of course, will be to adapt for the stage the dances these people may have performed in real life. These dances take on two classifications: contemporary ("social") and historical ("folk"). When dealing with contemporary time periods, such as the twentieth century, the decade being depicted is more important than the period's subcultural variations—after all, one would assume that a jitterbug in New York is the same as a jitterbug anywhere else. Cultural accents should be applied to the steps when dealing with historical eras, with dances of "entertainment" within a show (e.g., a nightclub scene), or with numbers establishing a special setting.

The dances of a certain region also reflect a moral code. The closeness and positioning of the bodies, the placement and use of arms and hands, the treatment of the partner, and the movement patterns themselves will indicate the culturally predominant male-female relationship.

Try not to get carried away with the fruits of cultural research. While accuracy is the aim, entertainment is the ultimate goal. For example, folk dances, as a rule, are not designed to be theatrical or climactic pieces in real life. Frequently, they simply begin with the music and keep going until the music stops. There is no "beginning-middle-end" construction to follow, no gathered momentum or change of dynamic, and such numbers, if presented realistically on stage, would become boring for audiences after a short time.

The theatrical styles of other cultures must also be adapted to whatever country or culture the show will be presented in. A prime example is the "Small House of Uncle Thomas" ballet from *The King and I.* The use of theater in Siam was quite the opposite from what Westerners today would expect in a musical comedy. Whereas we attend theater to seek some catharsis or great emotional release, the Eastern approach is to soothe and relax the viewer. The slow, graceful turning, curling, and flexing movements of the limbs, coupled with the shimmering reflections of hundreds of tiny mirrors and jewels sewn into the costumes, produce a hypnotic, peaceful state of being. Even chase scenes and battles are presented in slow motion in the dances. Yet such an interlude in the middle of a three-hour musical would numb the Western mind, and destroy the pace of the show.

TOPICAL/HISTORICAL EVENTS

The final area of research is that of topical/historical events. What was the state of the world at the time of the original production's success? Didn't *Oklahoma!* give a wartime United States a much-needed shot of Americana? *On the Town* was certainly a frolic in uniform. And didn't the circumstances of *South Pacific* strike a chord with the postwar returnees in 1949? The gang wars of the '50s gave birth to *West Side Story*, and the Elvis Presley phenomenon was parodied in *Bye Bye Birdie*. Pop Art of the early '60s later resulted in *It's a Bird, It's a Plane, It's Superman*, and *Hair* in 1967 was *the* statement of the hippie revolt.

What was the state of musical theater when the show first appeared? Were there popular trends in format or structure? Was the show written to promote a contemporary idea or performer? What was its competition that season, especially if it was nominated for, or won, any theatrical awards?

In the case of any musical, authentic staging is a matter of continuing an endeavor already started by others. Without knowing what has gone before or understanding the background of a specific show, there will not be much input on which to base one's staging effort. The result will be an "inappropriate" production, seemingly created in a vacuum.

GLOSSARY:

BASIC DANCE TERMS

arabesque   the position in which the body is supported by one leg, flexed or locked, while the other leg is extended back as fully as possible. Both legs and feet are usually in a turned-out position.

assemblé   a small jump in which the legs, from toe to thigh, are straightened and brought together in the air, and that finishes with both feet landing at the same time.

attitude   a term describing a bent leg that is extended in the air, while the body is supported by one flexed or locked leg; the leg in attitude may be extended either in front or back.

ball change   a tap dance term for the two sounds made as a dancer steps quickly from the ball of one foot to the ball of the other and back again.

barre   the wooden railing found in most dance studios, especially those devoted to classical ballet, at which warm-up exercises are executed.

battement   a leg swing in which the working leg moves freely from the hip forwards, sideways, or backwards, only as high as the body naturally allows. While the working leg always has the knee locked, the supporting leg may be flexed or straight. A **grande battement** is created by swinging the leg as high as possible.

body roll   frequently used as a warm-up exercise, body rolls may be done in different variations but all include a collapse—bending of the knees, lowering of head and full curving over of the spine—and then a straightening movement starting from the knees and moving up through the thighs, hips, spine, and head.

coupé   literally meaning "cut," the term refers to the short, incisive movement of the feet where one foot is moved away and the other quickly takes its place.

degagé   the word comes from the French word that refers to the lifting of the foot from the floor, most often while pointed.

demi-plié   a slight bending of the knees while the rest of the body remains still. **Pliés** are done in all five leg positions; **grand pliés** are deep knee bends and in certain positions the heels rise from the floor.

developpé   the slow unfolding of the working leg from a bent knee position through to an **arabesque**. The supporting leg may be either flexed or locked.

flap   one of the most basic tap steps, it is created by relaxing the ankle and flicking the ball of the foot at the floor and then stepping onto the same foot thereby producing two quick sounds. A **flap-heel** makes three sounds by dropping the heel right after the flap.

frappé   literally, the term means to "hit" or "strike" and it refers to a dancer tapping the floor with the ball of the foot without changing the height of the bent knee so all movement comes from the ankle. Frappés are often performed as warm-up exercises at the barre and may be done to the front, back, and side.

glissade   a gliding, traveling step, where one leg moves laterally and the other leg closes to meet it.

glissées   a series of barre or warm-up exercises where the dancer lets the working foot glide along the floor in a light, sweeping motion until the pointed toe moves slightly into the air. They are done to the front, back, and side, and either in turned-out or parallel positions.

hip lift   the raising of one hip forward, backward, or to the side.

hitch kick   a scissor-like kick made by the quick switching of the legs in the air.

isolations   one of the most distinguishable features of jazz dance, the term refers to the independent movement of any one part of the body—shoulder, elbow, hips, head—in a separate, "isolated" action.

jazz hand   a hand posture in which the palm faces forward and the fingers are spread.

jazz split   a move where the dancer slides to the floor with the front leg extended and locked and the rear leg bent—a position that resembles that of a track hurdler. The same hand as the forward leg breaks the fall while the other arm and hand is extended overhead.

jazz square   a four-step movement wherein the dancer travels laterally, crossing one foot over the other, steps backwards, then back across, and finally forward to the point of origin.

jeté   the classic ballet term for a leap from one leg to another.

Labanotation   one of the most widely accepted systems for notating and recording dance movement on paper, it is named after its inventor Rudolf Laban (1879–1958).

opposition   refers to simultaneous body movements that are diametrically opposite. The most obvious example occurs during normal walking—one arm swings forward while the other swings back, so the arms are said to be in "opposition."

parallel   the placement of the feet and legs so the front-to-back line for each limb does not intersect with the other; the position is used frequently in modern and jazz dance as an alternative to the "turned-out" positions of classical ballet.

pas de deux   any dance performed by a couple.

pirouette   a 360-degree spinning turn executed in place on one leg, either flexed or straight; the exact kind of pirouette is defined by the other working leg which, like the arms, may be in a wide range of positions.

port de bras   a classical ballet term that refers to the positioning or carriage of the arms.

prance   a hopping movement executed either in place or, more frequently, as a means of travel, created by straightening the supporting leg as the other leg moves forward, and is lifted, bent at the knee in attitude, with the foot usually pointed.

pull-backs   a slightly advanced tap move made by rocking from the heel to the toe, slapping or spanking the floor with the toe, pulling back the foot, and then stepping on the same foot—all while the other foot is in the air. Most frequently, the move is performed as a **double pull-back** resulting in four sounds, two for each spank and two for each foot's step.

relevé   the lifting of the body up onto half-toe by raising the heels.

rond de jambe   a rotating motion of a leg that may be done in a variety of positions, either toward or away from the body.

scuff   a single tap sound made by lifting and sliding the foot forward on the floor.

seat spin   a turn done in a sitting position, knees most often drawn up to the chest, and feet flexed or pointed; the spinning motion is provided by one hand that pushes the floor.

shuffle   one of the basic tap dance steps, the shuffle creates two sounds by lightly flicking the toe tap back and forth on the floor. Unlike the **flap**, the foot ends up in the air. A **shuffle-step** combination would create a third sound with the placement of the foot on the floor after the shuffle.

sissonne   a jump in which the dancer lands on one foot with the other extended either to the front, back, or side.

stag leap   a leap distinguished by the front leg which is bent at the knee, toe pointed toward, and almost touching the knee of the back leg.

tendu   the stretching of the leg, moving from a closed to an open position, with the toe never leaving the ground. This movement is most often done as a warm-up exercise and may be executed to the front, back, and side.

INDEX

ABOUT THE AUTHOR

The late Robert Berkson, stage name of Robert Berger, received a B.S. degree from Emerson College in 1971, and studied at the Boston School of Ballet and Boston Conservatory. He choreographed and/or directed over 40 musicals on all theatrical levels, both amateur (community, high school, university) and professional (summer stock, dinner theater, opera, and touring companies). While acting as artist-in-residence at Harvard University, he taught classes in tap, jazz, and musical comedy dance styles, and choreographed a production of *West Side Story* with Leonard Bernstein as advisor.

Mr. Berkson directed and choreographed an extensive international tour of *Hair* which ran for several years. He also served as production supervisor and artistic coordinator for productions of *West Side Story* in Madrid, Algiers, Vienna, Rio de Janeiro, and Tel Aviv.

From 1980 to 1985, he was a director for the J.H. Cargill Producing Organization. Robert Berkson died in September, 1986.